THE POETIC DOCUMENTARY:
FROM JORIS IVENS TO NONNY DE LA PEÑA

Dr. Alexandru Vlad
CLUJ-NAPOCA
2021

CONTENTS

About the Author 6

Introduction 7

1. Aesthetics of fine arts and its influences on the poetic documentary 11

1.1. Byzantine aesthetics, the Middle Ages, the Renaissance, and the poetic documentary 31

1.2. Mannerism, Baroque, Classicism and Rococo: the pathway to modern aesthetics 37

1.3. Aesthetics of modern art 40

1.4. Visual arts at the end of the 19th century and the transition to film art 44

1.5. Digital age and conversion to global culture 48

2. Foray into the history of documentary film from the perspective of aesthetics 51

2.1. The birth of a new aesthetic 52

2.2. The film of political propaganda and its relationship with the poetic mode 60

2.3. The maturation of aesthetics 74

2.4. Modern documentaries and the issue of contemporary aesthetics 84

3. Aesthetics and genres of documentary film 93

3.1. The origin and evolution of poetic documentaries 99

3.2. The transition to exhibition documentaries 104

3.3. The poetic, the observational, and the participatory 110

3.4. Where the aesthetics of the poetic documentary meets the reflexive 124

3.5. The performative or the mode closest to the poetic 129

3.6. Experimental film, visual essay, or poetic documentary 135

4. Poetic documentary: another way of visual expression 141

4.1. Symbolism in poetic documentary 158

4.2. The directorial vision - an aesthetic of cyclicity 163

4.3. Global interconnection 167

4.4. Narrative structure in poetic documentary 173

4.5. Timing and time.. 178

4.6. Sound and music.. 182

4.7. Image 186

5. Poetic documentary and future film trends 197

5.1. The concepts of cloud filmmaking and VR from the perspective of poetic documentaries 203

5.1.1. Movie review: Waves of Grace............... 208

5.2. Interactive documentaries and their connection with the aesthetics of the poetic mode 211

5.2.1. Conversational mode 215

5.2.2. Hypertext mode 220

5.2.3. Participatory mode 222

5.2.4. The experimental mode 225

Conclusions 230

Bibliography 235

Filmography 253

Other video resources 258

About the Author

Alexandru Vlad works in the cinematography industry as a documentary director and finished his Ph.D. in 2019 at Babeș-Bolyai University in Cinematography and Media Field. He won the "Special Mention" (DocuArt Festival, 2014) and in 2015 he was nominated in the category of "Best Documentary Short Film" at Gopo Awards, Romania, as director of Another Day of Mankind (2014), and he received "Best Picture of Documentary Film" Award (International Film Festival and Slideshow Autumn at Voronet, 2015). In 2016, he won the "Best Director of Documentary Film" Award with the We Fly Again project (Festivalul Internațional de Film și Diaporamă Toamnă la Voroneț, 2016) In 2020 he won the prize from the Organisation internationale de la Francophonie, his projects being elected in over 50 official selections in film festivals from our country and from abroad. Presently, he works also as a professor of the "Cercul de Film-TV", at the Children's Palace in Cluj-Napoca, Romania, while he is also actively involved in the scientific research of the film documentary and of the new technologies with which it interacts.

Introduction

Ever since the invention of video cameras, filmmakers have tried to determine the potential of this mode of visual expression, realizing that its great asset is the faithful reproduction of reality. As Bazin emphasizes in his work What is cinema?, the real exists in the film in the form of pure reality, created by expressiveness and essence, also in pseudo-real form, generating the viewer's disappointment through editing tricks, directing, scenography, etc. (Bazin 15).

Although documentaries are one genre that wants to represent reality as faithful as possible, few theorists are interested in the theoretical aspects of this cinematic category. Among the enthusiasts of this subject, we can mention Paul Rotha and Bill Nichols. Studying their bibliography, together with other theorists, we discover that the focus of their research falls more on the documentary structures, the relationship they have with the social space, the limitations as a genre or ethical issues; less of the aesthetic ones. This research project, on the aesthetics of the poetic documentary, is proposed to analyze the evolution of the genre and to highlight the fundamentals that arise in various stages of cinema development. Such a study is very important because, without deep research of how the poetic documentary has developed from an aesthetic point of view, it is almost impossible to specify the impact it has on the development of societies and cultures globally.

Well-known film critic Mark Cousins states that the documentary is, through the number of frames (rhythm, structure, etc.), as complex as the fiction film. Also, during an April 22, 2010 interview at the American University of Michigan, film director Sergio Basso and sociologist Daniele Cologna argue that through the film there is no direct-fundamental connection with the real world, because any objectivity recorded with the help of the camera it is only a representation, consequently an artificial product by its very nature (Bonsaver 304).

Another important aspect brought up during the interview is the existence of the documentary as an independent genre. Apart from the observational mode (as defined by Bill Nichols), other types of documentaries tend to incorporate particular aesthetic features of other genres of film or audiovisual products (animation, fiction, experimental, etc.).

Andrei Gorzo emphasizes the realistic character of the documentaries, recalling in his book Lucruri care nu pot fi spuse altfel, the film Nanook of the North (1922), more precisely the sequences in a full shoot in which the life of the Eskimo's is documented. The lack of fragmentation by editing the scenes supports the continuity of the real

(Lucruri care nu pot fi spuse altfel 50). What Gorzo does not specify, however, is the fact that a large part of the scenes of this documentary was directed with the help of script elements, scenery, and lights artificially introduced in the film, as Ted Mills notes in his chronicle. On the other hand, "the observation by participation and the resumption in front of the camera of the gestures or habits of some characters brings as much veracity and authenticity as the surprise recorded with the hidden camera" (Damian 16).

Another theory that underlies the expository mode is found in Lucian Maier's study from the book Politicile filmului, where we are informed that, although the expository documentaries (such as those produced by Discovery, BBC, Viasat) have a wide range of spread and popularity, "the way it addresses the viewer should arouse high susceptibility" (Maier 219). That the information is presented along the way as being "verified" by competent people creates for the viewer the illusion of absolute truth, which can be assimilated without appeal. Besides, how information is filtered in an expository documentary highlights a lack of objectivity.

The image of the omniscient author is dismantled by Gorzo in his book Imagini încadrate în istorie. It presents Cristi Puiu's conclusion on Michael Moore's documentary, which emphasizes the unprofessional attitude that the documentary filmmaker displays, by putting the characters interviewed in a bad light (Imagini încadrate în istorie 15).

We find the same argument in the documentary Autobiography of Nicolae Ceaușescu, in which Ujică associates the archive images through a sarcastic montage, with an ironic soundtrack, therefore distorting the string of reality (Imagini încadrate în istorie 15). Following these theories suggested by the listed critics and film authors, we recognize the versatile direction of the theories regarding the documentary film. This divergent exposition of criticism pops up throughout the historical evolution of the genre, involving solid research to determine the aesthetic direction in which the documentary is presently maturing.

1. Aesthetics of fine arts and its influences on the poetic documentary

This chapter aims to illustrate the current theories on aesthetics, with the application at the level of visual arts (history, definitions, classifications, elements, etc.), and the definition of the meaning behind the visual structures used in the film, especially in the poetic documentary film. The impact and importance of the birth of new symbols and executive concepts important for the evolution of documentary film throughout history will also be followed.

Research of elements in the field of aesthetics generates a context helpful to the documentation of episodic phenomena or less visible in the poetic documentary. I will insist on the end of the chapter in particular on the key elements that generate a cinematic language focused on symbolism and visual elements. Attention will fall on certain cultures or historical periods at the expense of others, priority being those relevant to the conceptual and argumentative development of the present work.

To best summarise the relationship between the aesthetics of the visual arts and that of the documentary film, it is important to see how aesthetics are defined.

Aesthetics are the fundamental elements of the arts, without which the shape of the artistic product cannot be shaped. According to the dictionary of the specialized, aesthetics is defined as "the philosophical discipline that studies the essence, laws, categories, and structure of that human attitude towards reality, characterized by the reflection, contemplation, valorization, and creation of specific features of objects and processes in nature, society, and consciousness or human (artistic) creations." (Achim et al. 110).

The term aesthetics comes from the Greek language, specifically from the word aisthesis, meaning something that can be perceived with the help of the senses. Aesthetics has been developing since its inception as a branch of philosophy, being circumscribed terminologically and conceptually by the German philosopher A. G. Baumgarten in 1750 in the work Aesthetica, written in Latin.

Undoubtedly, aesthetics, a fundamental discipline for the advancement of art, comes as support for an indisputable understanding of its standards in general. Aesthetics in the visual arts is contextualized as a way of maximizing efficiency in the communication of messages through images, compositions, rhythm, perspectives, and movements. At the same time, this dimension can be easily applied both in the analysis and in the synthesis of materials that are part of the video arts.

Theoretical concepts of media aesthetics are constantly used for encoding and decoding the audiovisual message assembly. Thus, our attention is directed to the semiotics and hermeneutics involved in this process. The message propagation environment is always a command center in making the ratio between form and content more efficient.

As Daniel Chandler states: "the term environmental is used by different theorists and may include boundary categories such as speech, writing or any other technical form related to the media" (Chandler, Semiotics for Beginners). This simple wording draws our attention to the polysemia of the concept of "environment" and inspires us to try to be very prudent in its use.

Theorists often associate each environment according to the communication channel involved and the senses they sharpen. They also point out that the study of the semiotic scan can make us more conscious about reality as a construction and of the role played by us and others in its construction. Meaning is not passed on to us, we generate it actively compared to a complex inner game of codes or conventions (Chandler, Semiotics for Beginners). Just as the semiconductor looks at the meaning in detail, hermeneutics synthesizes the concept of meaning in the macro-cosmic plane.

Going back to the set of elements that define aesthetics, we find space and time as primordial elements. The perspective applied to space can be of several kinds respecting one, two, three points, etc. For an image to be read identically to a clone of reality, it must be viewed exactly from the angle from which the perspective was imagined and conceived.

In addition to its technical role, color induces the viewer to certain states according to the code of the cultural paradigm in which it ends up being utilized.

The most common colors have a standard social precept, while specific colors could contextualize a general mood or idea. These meanings often do not go beyond the limit of the society that founded the meaning. An example is black color (or noncolor, in Newtonian spectrum terms), which often represents death in Western society while in eastern cultures white is used to symbolize death (Faur).

The meanings constructed by the set of lines, dots, and spots are defined with the applied aesthetics. Each society and culture is penciled in a specific paradigm of aesthetics, in general. The lines, in their sense, do not exist in nature, just as there are no points or stains. They occur in the form of optical phenomena created when the group of objects moves away from the viewer.

Movement, as an aesthetic element in all visual arts, is one of the most important general characteristics, whether we refer to the movement of the camera in audiovisual or to the movement suggested by the lines of perspectives and forms. Camera movements are used to describe spaces, actions, track characters, and generate emotions. They are classified according to the directions of the dynamics engaged in several categories.

The movements of characters and objects are more about the semiotics or hermeneutics of the landmark culture.

Rhythm is used in the visual arts to develop drama or to stress certain states or ideas. It is usually built on music and the images being cut at the exact moment when the sound resumes a passage or changes.

These elements mentioned above are some elements of the visual language, but also means of plastic, visual, cinematic, or artistic expression used in the construction of the images to which we will refer during the present work.

The evolution of documentary film and fiction film is closely linked to the evolution of aesthetics, found throughout the history of fine arts. How the visual arts grown is characterized by a selection of values that audiences and artists considered being essential in the development of art.

Since the beginning of the development of visual aesthetics as a formal concept, the theoretical foundation peaked especially in the 18th century (Kristeller 499). Art was classified as "something that cannot be taught or learned" (Kristeller 498). The difficulty of using visual language creatively has been and is amplified by the limitations we have at the time of creation. The materials used, the techniques, the tools, whether we are talking about digital visual arts or traditional ones, produce barriers that, more often than not, we hardly bypass in the creative process. These barriers have positioned artists on various professional levels throughout the history of the visual arts.

Aesthetic problems were manifested not only by physical limitations but also by the set of obstacles generated by the socio-cultural dimension of the reference period; beliefs, ideals, a vision of life were the basis of the conception of the visual arts. Including the status of the artist in society, elevated to a higher rank only during the Renaissance was and is a determining factor in terms of the quality that art can achieve. One of the basic concepts on which the visual arts (and not only) were based is a reproduction (Kristeller 504), the ancient problem of artistic representation.

We see nature as the first source of inspiration that man, the "measure of all things" as Protagoras synthesizes, harnesses it through cognitive processes, and uses it to meet his increasingly diverse needs. So the imitation of nature, this inexhaustible source of inspiration, becomes a common practice, and man appeals to all the means at his disposal. This is also the original concept under which cinema began if we remember punctually the films of the Lumière brothers, which captured pieces of life in the form of one-minute snapshots.

Imitation of nature or reality is a practice often found in the construction of documentary films. As we know, there are genres and subgenres dedicated only to reproduce the real, seeking an active observation of society through a neutral approach, distanced from the subject. For example, in the elaboration of observational documentaries, the real is defined in the form of a recording supposedly unaltered by the director. The neutrality of the relationship between subject and camera, and the lack of non-diegetic sounds, try to draw the viewer into the mirage of a simulacrum of reality. We are aware, as spectators, that what we see in these audiovisual products is only a simulation, and we know that the camera and the film crew in these documentaries inevitably put their mark on the recorded reality, especially since many of the observational documentaries are not just pure observation, but involve the arrangement of the décor, possibly the lights and even the recording of several doubles.

During poetic documentaries, we often encounter the real as a subjective representation, assumed by the film crew who try through the chosen techniques to introduce us to a world of experiences, experiences, and emotions that reality integrates into its spatial-temporal unfolding.

We, therefore, have this art of imitation which not only refers to forms imitated by the techniques of the plastic artists of Antiquity but also shows us that the imitation of nature has continuity in thousands of years. As we will see in the next chapters, virtual reality, augmented, 4D, 7D, or immersive technology are the modern steps that our society takes in imitating reality to provide a true simulation.

Because I had raised the term "ideal" in the social perception of the time, this ideal was often defined by the term "beautiful" (Aslam 5). But beauty is a subjective aspect that has changed its paradigm with socio-cultural transformations. Today's beauty is much different from ancient beauty in terms of the appearance of the proportions of the human body, the appearance of clothing, interior design, architecture, sculpture, painting, etc.

In connection with what the Greek population considered beautiful, an important step in the evolution of aesthetics was bringing into focus the person and the human body. The deities receive human face and stature, physical and character weaknesses and – in a moment of fundamental social, political and cultural structuring – a man not only reaches the top of the food pyramid but also becomes aware of his status as a being capable of conceiving the entire future of the universe.

Attention to the human body, human traits, as we will discover throughout Chapter 4, is an aspect intensely exploited by documentarians of the poetic way. If the observational documentary focuses on the relationships between beings and their surrounding universe, the human is revealed in poetic documentaries by playing sensory experiences. We cannot fail to mention The Act of Seeing with One's Own Eyes (1971), where Brakhage focuses this human sensory and emotional experience on the human body, the film becoming practically a metacognitive experiment of our bodily existence and the way we relate morally, emotionally and culturally to the subjective experience of morgue room exploration and brutal processes of dissecting corpses.

If we mentioned Brakhege's film, we cannot help but describe the position of beauty in the paradigm of aesthetics. As we well know, beyond feelings, beauty has a cultural character. Also, in Chapter 4, we will discover how certain elements representative of one society can have a different meaning in another society.

Roussel discusses in his work entitled Aesthetic Ideal the aspects defined by Alexander Gottlieb Baumgarten, also known as the "Father of Aesthetics" (Aslam 4). Aesthetics, in Roussel's view, cannot be limited to formal criteria such as proportion, functionality, and form, etc. (Roussel-Despierres 429).

On the other hand, aesthetics is a tool that can be used on art of the present or the past, without being able to plausibly anticipate a possible development of art in the future, it being a byproduct of artistic creation, which arose after the work of art was born (Aslam 14). We have selected all these hypotheses to open readers the horizon on the specifics and the problem of defining aesthetics throughout history.

The proportion, beyond the mathematical aspects in which the parts of the human body represent certain fractions of the whole, is characterized by a sum of principles. Policlet has devoted much of his intellectual work to the development of a treatise entitled Canon, on the exact proportions that define the beauty of the human body, but also symmetry as a defining principle (Celkyte).

Borrowed from the Egyptians, the principle of symmetry appears as a recurring factor in the culture of various historical periods that we can investigate. This principle is not only a theoretical side of aesthetics but also a determining factor derived from psychology, people being attracted to the face, body, or other elements that have characteristics specific to symmetry (Grammer and Thornhill 233). The phenomenon presented by

Grammer and Thornhill in their research sends us to the same hypothesis, namely that aesthetics and beauty are built around our subjective senses; therefore, they are not autonomous structures that can operate outside the individual self.

In democratic societies, the principle of asymmetry is preferably adopted in the territorial organization as a form of adaptation to nature, while dominant societies prefer symmetry as an artificial organization tool imposed on nature ("The Perspective in Ancient Greece").

"Symmetry, however, is not the only characteristic that defines beauty, with Aristotle stating that size is also necessary" (Celkyte). These statements are supported by examples such as the fact that it is not enough for a body or a city to be well proportioned to be beautiful, but a certain size (Celkyte) is also required.

The role of these analyses, however, is not only to discover the beauty of formal principles that define aesthetics but also to reflect on the fundamental purpose of art in society. Art, implicitly visual arts, presents itself throughout history as a reflection on human nature in the search for truth (Aslam 46).

Truth, in turn, is the root of morality. Aesthetics, having its independent moral norms, have been constantly compared to spiritual morality (Roussel-Despierres 431). Thus, the establishment of ideal proportions and symmetry are directly influenced by the spiritual universe and spiritual morality. For Greeks, art is the phenomenon that describes the soul of its creator (Roussel-Despierres 431).

With the emergence of what might be called Greek realism (ca. 500-330 B.C.) and democracy, at the expense of symmetry and artificialized proportions, Greek culture reaches its peak by imitating the real ("Greek Sculpture"). This shows us that, although aspirations towards a utopian ideal of proportions and symmetry carefully constructed in the philosophy of past times have remained fundamental, Greek artists are at the same time aware of the limitations that human nature has, a consciousness reflected in the realistic character of their art, stemming from the imitation of nature. The world of the arts is a dream, a fantasy, an aspiration of man to perfection in a continuous struggle with the cosmic chaos that he tries to master through his divinized actions (Aslam 47).

The spirit or creative self from which the work of art emerges and essentially the discourse about the aesthetics does not show up in an infinite form in ancient Greece, as we are used to appearing in the representations of contemporary cultures, but manifests itself spontaneously in a natural form, a sensual existence (Hegel and Bryant 147). But we must not ignore that the ultimate purpose of art during this period was not entirely decorative or simply the expression of the creator's philosophy, but was likewise to educate or ennoble society ("The Meaning of Greek Art"), providing it a "manual" of aesthetic and moral conduct. Beyond proportion, it also reflects the size of the beauty in the work's functionality of art (Celkyte). The theory of functional beauty is formed around the idea that beauty also comes from the object's ability to achieve its predestined functions (Celkyte).

In the documentary film, beauty is present both in the form prescribed by our contemporary culture and in the ability of images to connect and develop meanings. A convenient example is The Wonderful, Horrible Life of Leni Riefenstahl (1993). Since the beginning of the film, we have a succession of underwater frames representing divers exploring a coral reef, alternated with images from Nazi Germany and other archival images from the life of director-actress Leni Riefenstahl. Although images of the coral reef have in our cultural conception a meaning linked with beauty, in the aesthetics of poetic documentary the alternating frames of the director's intimate life (the dance of the African tribe, for example) are full of emotions that define the beautiful beyond the explicit (physical) characteristics. Beauty becomes a human universe, existential, through sensory experienced reality.

The form of beauty involves a didactic function, as Celkyte states: "It is stated that a lover first falls in love with an individual body, then discovers that there is a community between all beautiful bodies and then turns into an admirer of the human form." All these theories lead us to whether the ancient art that we subject to an analytical quest today is the art that the theorists of the period are talking about.

"Contemporary art has taught us that aesthetics do not always involve beauty. We can still think about the aesthetics of nature, which is exploring how nature is observed. My claim is that the perception of art turns into meaning, even if that meaning is not translatable into verbal form, as opposed to watching nature that provides us an experience of beauty or the sublime."

(Erzen 1)

Many of the works that have been saved are copies done by Roman artists after the original Greek works (Hemingway and Hemingway). It is important to note that when we carry out a comprehensive study of the era, we must take this into account and how it affects the quality of our analysis.

Let's go back to one of the essential issues I mentioned sooner, which is mimesis or the art of imitation. So we see that copying is not just about copying or imitating nature. Imitation can also be made by reproducing works of art, objects created by man, etc. We usually adopt this phenomenon in contemporary works in situations where, through the art of collage, digital manipulations, etc., certain works of art or mundane objects are transformed into other artistic products in a new physical or conceptual form. The rule of imitation is often described as an image "understood as involving not only copying but also creative interpretation" (Celkyte). We deduce that, in the view of that time, the concept of imitative representation pursues precisely the subjective appearance of reality. We, then, have a direct analogy with the aesthetic functions of a poetic documentary. The subjective perspective in which the poetic documentary is hidden becomes the dominant theme of the respective representational mode.

In Greek art we discussed previously, the artist assumes a certain representation of the real at the expense of other representations such as a certain position of the human body, animal, or other situations. Besides this aspect, the artist willingly or unwillingly omits certain elements displayed in reality, and in the depiction's case of objects already represented, "the products of artistic activities are criticized for having twice been subjected to omissions towards the element from which he is inspired. Socrates uses the example of a banquet couch to argue that painting a sofa is just a copy of reality. However, the real sofa made by the craftworker is also only a copy of the true reality, of the forms" (Celkyte).

The poetic documentary is not limited to reproducing a certain position, shape, color. He seeks to manage his temporal dimension as intensely as possible to delineate us from the experiences and elements that make us not see the subjective reality imagined by the director. We can also discuss how perspective is rendered and how images are often intentionally distorted to destroy natural realism, at the expense of experiments and psychological effects.

The linear perspective had not yet been developed in Antiquity. The ancient Greeks and Romans used various tricks to represent depth in the visual space. For example, in the case of theatre, the scenographic elements were painted or illuminated in such a way as to produce the illusion of depth in space ("Greek Art theory and style" 5).

We see that illuminating or coloring the different elements of scenography to achieve the feeling of perspective is a practice adopted since Antiquity. Later, it would develop into a model in modern painting (see Henri Matisse), but also in experimental film. This quality has been adopted by the directors of poetic documentaries, even if light and color are not used simply for the rendering of perspective, but have a higher complex role in defining the visual space, as in Stan Brakhage's film, Stellar (1993).

To discover the spatial perspective used in Ancient Greece, I will give as an example some clarifications from the work of Mary the Future, because it is one of the most relevant descriptions of the phenomenon. The perspective in Ancient Greece was represented originally in the form of a two-point perspective or an open axial view, "resulting from the change of architectural compositions to relief and a long exercise of visual perception" (Urmă 1).

The two-point perspective, according to Professor Maria Urmă, was accomplished "by the oblique access of roads among the monuments and by the elimination of the main objects of the architecture within the central axis of the gaze or by placing entrances in the corners of the markets as main points of view" (Urmă 4).

As for the perspective with the axial view described by Urmă, it applies to the channeling of attention with the help of architectural elements to an open space where there is frequently a natural element, an opening of landscape, or perhaps an architectural element (10).

We should not forget that the linear perspective and other types of perspectives adopted, despite their usefulness, were subsequently neglected by modern artists at the expense of the overturned perspective or other types of perspectives. We recall this fact to restore attention to the complexity of the factors that contribute to the definition and circumscription of aesthetics in the conception of the ancient Greeks.

Color in Ancient Greece plays an important role in defining visual shapes and symbols. The first words describing colors are found in all ancient civilizations in the Middle East or the Mediterranean (Warburton 1-3). According to Osborne's work (1), colors can be organized in three ways:

1. Surface colors present on the surfaces of objects, taking the corresponding texture.

2. Film colors, artificial by nature, do not take the form of an object but are generated by a projection.

3. Volume colors are the colors we experience when we look through a glass of red wine, a colored smoke, or a cloud, colors that have "the third dimension".

Using certain pigments of color depended very much on the cost of manufacturing, so certain colors such as purple or gold tent were used only by wealthy people and those with official status (Nenova). The color was used for the decoration of statues, for fresco paintings (wall decoration), wood painting, of which today very few have been preserved, but besides these aspects, it was for the Hellenics and a way of exposing the social status

(Nenova). Following investigations, we discover the fulness of functionalities that color had in people's lives. All objects with decorative function were usually ornate in various colors that also had a special symbolism.

The pigments were got from iron oxide, various plants, clay, gypsum, limestone, which were used in various combinations and diluted with water ("Classical Colour Palette"). The color had, as it is today, a special symbolism, often used in the ancient culture to represent something in a simple and easily decoded way by the great mass of the population.

In the poetic documentary, color is not limited to describing a certain physical characteristic of an object and is often used as a symbol. For example, we encounter grey and brown tones in the scenes of films made by Ron Fricke (Samsara, Baraka), colors used to stress the reality of developing societies. As mentioned above, I will detail many of these aspects during the following chapters, which is why I do not think it applies to argue by several examples or by more explicit examples those mentioned.

In retrospect, the art of Antiquity leaves its mark on universal culture and brings to our attention even today, in a suite of variable and complex forms, its fundamental influences in the malleable process of cultural evolution.

1.1. Byzantine aesthetics, the Middle Ages, the Renaissance, and the poetic documentary

It is well known that with the end of Antiquity, practically of the classical period, the aesthetics of the fine arts have undergone a profuse transformation. The Byzantine period, marked by the scale that the Christian religion had gained, was the engine that led Western Europe a little later in the Renaissance.

As I mentioned in the previous sub-chapter, I will not dwell on a detailed description of these periods, but I will focus my attention on reviewing important aspects of the evolution of aesthetics, which will be used later to emphasize the connection and continuity with cinematic art.

Emperor Constantine the Great opens this chapter of history with the Battle of Milvian Bridge in 312 BC, where he defeats Maxentius and thus becomes the supreme ruler of the Roman Empire (Evans, Holcomb, and Hallman 5). The event applies to the importance of visual symbols in our culture, by using Christ's monogram in the form of a painting on the shields of soldiers, a vision that Emperor Constantine would have had before the battle and which would have brought victory to his army (Evans, Holcomb, and Hallman 5).

Christianity, through its symbols, becomes an important part of art history, making its mark on aesthetics. It is important to note how a wide part of the directors of the poetic documentary introduced the symbols of Christianity during the documentary films made (see Samsara, Baraka, Chronos, etc.), which is a theme often exploited together with the symbols and elements specific to other religions. The cathedral, the symbol of medieval Christianity, is present in the Chronos son as an immortal edify in the struggle with time, along with other architectural relics from various eras. The succession of days and nights over Christian architecture strengthens our thought of eternity and aesthetic continuity.

Towards the end of the 4th century, after the Christian religion becomes the official religion of the Roman Empire, a multitude of symbols appear both in the space inside the church and in the private spaces of the dwellings. Images of religious scenes, images of saints, or visual symbols such as lamb or pigeon are often encountered during this period. The emergence of the first Christian churches, the use of mosaics, and colors impose a new standard in the evolution of religious cults and their inspired representations.

The visual reforms of these times are harnessed by iconoclasm, the movement against icons started by Leon III through edicts drawn up between 726 and 729 (Evans, Holcomb and Hallman 7). We are also relieved by the second Council of Nicea, in 787, where iconoclasm is defeated and the cult of icons returns under a set of precise rules in the Eastern church (Tanner).

The second cycle of the glory of Byzantine art is marked by the outburst of visual arts, which uses fresh materials and techniques, from the use of ivory and precious stones to painting and mosaic. The Christian cult goes through a period of flowering and widespread (Evans, Holcomb, and Hallman 7).

The Middle Ages in the West are dominated, as Umberto Eco reminds us, by scholastic philosophy and the political instability of the Ages. The papacy's need to seek the military support of Charles the Great and his appointment as Roman Christian Emperor in 800 marked the beginning of the resurrection of European culture (Norris, Arkenberg, and Fluke 14).

Also known as the Carolingian Renaissance, this period of scientific and cultural progress was made possible by protecting culture by Charles the Great who set up schools besides monasteries and even a school at the royal court, called the Palatine School (Manea).

Painting depictions of biblical scenes and miniature-enriched manuscripts followed the course of economic prosperity, especially in the following period, during the reign of Otto I (Norris, Arkenberg, and Fluke 15). The first international aesthetic style, namely the Romanesque style, is born during the same period. It is followed in chronological order by the Gothic style. Their characteristics are widely known and we will not dwell on them.

Marking scientific progress through the transition stages from agrarian to the modern, technological economy is a recurring theme in both the fine arts and the documentary film. As we can see during the Qatsi trilogy, the world is presented in all these modern stages of transition. Just as the artists of the time in the Middle Ages immortalized the triumph of new inventions and their downfall, so the directors of poetic documentary films punctuated with the luxury of detail the modern era and its stages of evolution and decay.

I will also take a brief look at the important aspects that the Renaissance has promoted and developed with major historical events. We are talking about all the transformations that followed the 13th century, the stage when Europe is transitioning from an agrarian society to an urban society fuelled by international trade in goods and in which the birth of the middle class and its independence from the central powers: church and nobility (Raditsa, Arkenberg and Burnham 9) occur.

Humanism, the current that brought the human being into the midst of scientific and aesthetic research, inspired by the vision of Protagoras who states that "man is the measure of all things", imitates the style of great Roman writers like Cicero. We will observe in the following chapters, especially in Chapter 4, how the attention of a man and everything that derives from his universe falls to the consideration of the creators of the poetic documentary. We see, thus, that humanism is not limited to literature or painting. Its character, which tends towards universality, transcends the boundaries of classical artistic paradigms.

Art is growing based on social prosperity and technological progress focused on the development of vital inventions such as printing, which allows access to information much faster and at a substantially lower cost (Raditsa, Arkenberg, and Burnham 9). Man, therefore, becomes a center of interest for art spurred by classical writings and establishes himself as an active element in all narrative and aesthetic constructions.

Social, political, and religious reforms do not stop showing up. The world, in a continuous change, follows new techniques in the elaboration of paintings. The oil technique gradually replaces the other processes, becoming a standard in painting works. The sculpture is reborn under the chisel of new sculptors like Donatello, Michelangelo, Ghiberti from the schools and guilds established in Pisa and Florence.

At the beginning of this new trend, the linear and aerial perspective dominates the compositional structures. All their elements are arranged in such a way as to facilitate their private or group observation by the viewer (Raditsa, Arkenberg, and Burnham 12). The materials used are considered a unitary whole simultaneously with the composition and subject so that at the schools and guilds where the apprentices learned the secrets of the crafts the materials used were essential as the other elements (Raditsa, Arkenberg and Burnham 13).

I wanted to describe how society has changed concerning discoveries and inventions that emerged and developed during the Renaissance period because this continuous change and transformation is yet happening today inside the poetic documentary which tries to keep up with new technologies.

1.2. Mannerism, Baroque, Classicism and Rococo: the pathway to modern aesthetics

A series of artistic currents were built, developed, and disappeared in the centuries following the Renaissance, leading the way to modern art. The great social pressures imposed by the Church through anti-reform actions and inquisition have had a powerful impact on art ("Art of Renaissance and Baroque Europe"). These actions were manifested later (and even today) in societies where totalitarianism (and not only) prevailed or predominated. Censorship – religious, moral, political – was a scourge and limited both the capacity of filmmakers and the public. The aim of censorship was and is to "filter information, monitor publications, block manuscripts and intellectual products hostile to the regime" (Malita 9). The dissolution of the Censorship Institution in Romania was, according to Malița, only " an act of coarse manipulation – a real theatrical coup that allowed censorship to survive its own orchestrated disappearance (Malita 386). In various forms, crude or more subtle, it still exists today.

In 2009, Ronald Deibert, professor of political science at the University of Toronto and co-founder and one of the main investigators of the **OpenNet initiative,** and Evgeny Morzov, a student visitor to Stanford University and collaborator of the **New**

York Times, explains, that many of the companies in the United States, Finland, France, Germany, the UK, Canada, and South Africa are partially responsible for increasing the sophistication of online content filtering worldwide (Morozov 2011). While filtering software sold by internet security companies is mainly marketed to businesses and individuals who want to protect themselves and their employees and families, governments also use them to block what they consider sensitive information (Chadwick and Howard 330-331).

Back a few centuries ago, we notice that the Mannerists and the baroque swordsmen adapted Leonardo da Vinci's sfumato technique and built contorted images and shapes, with strong contrasts between warm tones and cold tones, light and dark tones. Art becomes a mirror of social fears and tension. We will see in this paper how these techniques of image construction were also used in film aesthetics to simulate various categories of emotions.

In the 18th century, the nobility enjoyed the special status and illusion of infinite prosperity. As a result, some visual artists compete to capture scenes of love and the cheerful life of the wealthy classes, a movement that is known as Rococo. However, the powerful spirit of historical legends and stories is reflected in the works of the classicists, who will influence the emergence of neoclassicism. Works performed with academic precision and rigorously in the observance of the rules of composition, come to be regarded as the highest quality standard, according to the critics of the period, similar to the rigor in which the expositive documentary was and is made, subjecting itself to the elements of cinematic language used from the beginning of the documentary and pursuing the same aesthetic.

The present foray into the pre-modern period shows us how the complexity of the living artistic phenomenon is often subject to clear rules and which artists, regardless of the artistic product produced, must follow so that their merchandise can be marketed, consumed, and appreciated by the public. We see how the expression "l'art pour l'art" used by Théophile Gautier becomes a secondary goal in a society governed by the principles of consumerism, but on these issues, we will return later.

1.3. Aesthetics of modern art

Modern art emerges with the great revolutions against the political classes and the industrialization of the production of goods. Neoclassicism, Romanticism, Realism, and Impressionism are the currents that have radically changed the Aesthetics of the visual arts. In a troubled historical context, European countries almost permanently in armed conflicts, revolutions, or street protests, open the way to artistic currents that can better describe her daily life and pulse ("Introduction to Romanticism"). The core of Romanticism was formed and developed in countries where Romance languages were not national languages, such as England or Germany ("Introduction to Romanticism"). Imagination was by the Romantics as the supreme quality of the human mind, as Baudelaire points out in the Salon of 1859 (Baudelaire 85).

The basic concept of the romantic current cannot be contained in a single definition or formula, since it appeared as a reaction to permanent change (Honour and Fleming 240-255).

Where neoclassical painters have opted for a representation directly proportional to universal truth or standards of representation without interpretation through the prism of their own emotions, romantics chose the other way, subjective representation (Honour and Fleming 255-

262), as with poetic documentaries. So we can talk about a romantic current made up of several styles, given the subjective way artists interpret certain historical events, and the historical consequences arising from them (Honour and Fleming 257-262).

The subjects dealt with in romantic art are characterized by the rise of man from the mundane to his independence, the proximity to higher freedom, and a divine existence (Hegel and Bryant 149). This conceptual approach is also found, a little later, in the author's cinema, where the writer-director becomes a subjective and universal creator, present at all stages of the film's production. Miracles and legends are integrated into visual works in a natural, realistic way, in the form of divine presences or interventions. Divinity does not appear as an absolute or ideal concept, as in the works of the ancient Greeks of the first period, but creeps into reality in various forms (Hegel and Bryant 150).

As a contrast to the romantic movement manifested in all sides of culture and the arts, realism appears as immortalization of events that are attributed to a moralizing purpose concerning the course of society (Honour and Fleming 255-262).

Dominated by reason, Realism was supported by the latest scientific discoveries and philosophical works inspired by the positivism of Auguste Comte (Honour and Fleming 255-262).

The return to raw reality reminds us of the Greek realism described in the first sub-chapter of this work. We see clearly that the return to nature, to the simulation of the real, is an equally current theme in modern art. This way of building Aesthetics will also be found in the film, especially in European cinema after the 1950s.

The short period of realism is followed by one of the most important artistic movements of modern art, namely Impressionism. As is well known, Impressionism appears as a reaction against the academic rigors to which the works of art were run at the time of their evaluation for exhibitions and openings. Focus on the visual impression that an image leaves on us, impressionists follow those details that a landscape or other scene impregnates in memory and that we stay with after we stop tracking the image. Looking at it from another perspective, it should be pointed out that the Impressionists used a particular scene only as a pretext to make a painting, the emphasis falling on contours, lines, contrasts, and other elements which, until that time, were not seen as elements more important than the subject itself (Schapiro 150-174).

Presented as a contrast of expositional or observational documentaries, the poetic documentary convinces the viewer with its simulated emotions, depending to a large extent on its aesthetic construction. So we see a careful correlation between the features of Impressionism and the poetic documentary in terms of methods of creating form.

1.4. Visual arts at the end of the 19th century and the transition to film art

We are approaching our period of interest recalling that with photography, the visual arts gained abstract characteristics. We cannot exactly determine the level of influence that photographic art has had on other art forms; many visual artists used the camera obscura and, later, the camcorder to capture different scenes that could later be transformed and manipulated into works of art using another representation medium (Marder). In the documentary film Tim's Vermeer (2013), directed by Raymond Joseph Teller, it is shown how in the works of Johannes Vermeer two types of effects occur: chromatic aberrations and depth of field, specific to photographic lenses not to the human eye, observations that undeniably emphasize the use of mechanical aids in the creative process (Teller).

We see that the technological nation of production and society on a large scale has also taken its toll on the form in which art appears to the public. The aesthetics of visual arts not only exhibit fundamental paradigm changes over time but also reverberate from alternative forms in previous forms. Cinema is born when technology becomes a side without which modern society is being unable to conceive of its existence. This art is the product of scientific discoveries, depending on technology and its evolution as the very existence of modern society.

Just as its inventors declared that "cinema is an invention without a future", it is also untrue that the film, throughout its short history, remains under the same aesthetic and language fundamentals. These foundations have changed much over time, following the great mutations in the sphere of the other arts, but also in the sphere of aesthetic discourse. Of course, there has always been a rift between theory and practice in the artistic field, but for the world of aesthetics to become an independent field of ethics and the theory of knowledge was possible only at the end of the 18th century which influenced the artistic practice itself.

So at the beginning of mass cinema (Hollywood, 1920), we see how the emphasis in the construction of films falls on narrative structures and the effect on the audience (Bordwell, "The Art Cinema as a Mode of Film Practice" 60-62). We are already talking about a cinema that uses certain standards in terms of sequential editing, three-point lighting, shooting angles, use of different lenses, etc. (Bordwell, "The Art Cinema as a Mode of Film Practice" 60-62).

From the viewer's perspective, the perception of the art form will arise from the clues present in the artistic product and past experiences (Bordwell and Thompson 335). So, in the perception of the cinematic form, the audience must be prepared to discover certain clues and formal signs. Emotions also play an important role in the perception of form: in their work, Bordwell and Thompson show to us by a simple example how form can be perceived differently by reporting to the same situation in two different ways (Bordwell and Thompson 369). A man who sprains a leg can provoke an empathetic reaction with his state of pain, but if in the next frame we see a group making fun of his grief, we are likely to have fun as spectators (Bordwell and Thompson 381).

Although the film montage has led to a real revolution, especially in European cinema (and we refer here especially to the intellectual montage that appeared in Russia in the period after the Bolshevik revolution when the cultural production had not yet become entirely dogmatized), we recognize that this function, to compose a work of art, is not specific to the film, it is found in various plastic currents and not only (Bordwell, "The Picture of Montage in Soviet Art and Film" 10).

The emotions we process when watching a film, therefore, come from a world of montage, where shapes complement each other in a unified whole to create the illusion of reality, as Bordwell points out in The Art Cinema as a Mode of Film Practice. The meaning is also built in such a way as to ensure continuity in a broader form. Of course, as we see in Bordwell's work, the meaning is always related to public culture. If the public cannot recognize certain historical periods or certain peculiarities, it is likely that the original meaning, conceived by the director, will take another form in the minds of the spectators.

1.5. Digital age and conversion to global culture

How we can define the documentary film and its aesthetics in global culture and digitalization is probably the fundamental question of this work and to which we will try, in our research, to answer as elaborately as possible. This is even more so because, in the digital age, problems like the narrative line, which we have discussed succinctly previously, become eclipsed by many other seemingly more modern aspects (Manovic). In this new era, the very nature of the film is called into question, as long as the characters, sets, and lights can be simulated in a virtual environment (Manovic).

How we theorists will relate to this phenomenon is equally complicated to define, given that the common elements of classical films, such as the putting in filmed images of stories, are no longer an industry-standard (Manovic).

We bring up the evolution of documentary film, specifically documentary in the digital age, and remember how the classical aesthetics of the documentary film are designed into a set of graphic elements linked by programmed elements so that passaging a documentary film story is interactive. Several websites such as interactivedocumentary.net, arte.tv, aljazeera.com, pbs.org, etc. host interactive documentary films, giving them free of charge to the viewers. Thus, the content is divided between several means of transmitting information as graphic diagrams, games, video images, texts that braid take on the role of classical aesthetics, but also of the elements discussed above. These are just a few examples; sure that the modern documentary does not stop at this form. We have a whole series of hybrid genres, from docufiction to poetic documentary, which will be discussed at length in the next chapters.

Thanks to the freedom gained by documentary creators, we have a wide range of films today. With the maturation of the independent film and television publishing such material, they – however, varied formally – had huge commercial success (Daniels). We are now talking about the documentaries of Michael Moore, Davis Guggenheim, or Morgan Spurlock who not only reach a wide audience through their simple and logical way of following a structure of ideas but also cause certain TV stations to form their program with materials made in the same aesthetic code (Daniels).

The fast and minimally resourced way to create audiovisual content has enabled the democratization of documentary film through online distribution platforms, offering free or for a fee any material, regardless of country of origin or related budget. The film into the digital age is transforming by the day and we will see, in the following, these transformations in the world of documentary film.

New technologies allow us to experience other people's stories, dramas, or successes, facilitating our engagement in the cinematic universe.

The experience becomes more interactive than with classical cinema, where our interaction with technology and the environment represented is limited. The public's interest in experiencing emotions is the engine that draws the language and aesthetics of poetic documentary towards integration into the sphere of modern audiovisual products. Thus, the perspective of the poetic documentary in this digital age is surrounded by success, even if the poetic documentary in its traditional form undergoes fundamental changes of structure, content, and form. The issues listed briefly above, about the evolution of production, post-production, and distribution technologies, will be repeated in our research during Chapter 5 where we will analyze, the evolution and future trends of the poetic documentary.

2. Foray into the history of documentary film from the perspective of aesthetics

We must emphasize that in the realization of this chapter will be used the method of content analysis, applied to several documents, films, or scientific articles, to arrive at the structuring of the information in chronological order.

I would also like to take our analysis of the meeting of the documentary with the essay and poetry, beyond the concerns of the answer to the question - however - important "what is a poetic documentary?", In a complex and generative space that is built following, rather, the questions "what kind of reality" or "whose reality is represented?".

Our research will document the course of the genre from the first public screening of the film, made on December 28, 1895, going through the fight against the predominance of the consumption area fueled by the desire for maturation, and the actual maturation of the documentary. The research aims at the diegetic world of the documentary film, both from a historical point of view and of specialized criticism, to shed light on knowledge, current theories, and some fertile research perspectives for the future.

2.1. The birth of a new aesthetic

The first moments of the cinema's existence find it in an area of experimentation of the technical capacity made available to humanity by its creators. So, the cinema is born in a cafe in Paris, where hundreds of passers-by gather in amazement to see the "wonder" that would change our history forever. It is the year 1895; the year in which our entire existence, of film lovers, would be shaped/remodeled by the invention of the Lumière brothers. This device called cinématographe by its creators can film and project movies in 4: 3 format, black and white, with a duration of 50 seconds (Corciovescu and Râpeanu 14).

Shortly after the first public screening of a collage of such films made on December 28, 1895, the cinema began to take shape as a new and profitable industry. All the films produced by the Lumière company at that time were called newsreels and represented short, unprocessed fragments of reality. Among the most famous films of this kind, which can be seen even today, constituting precious documents of cultural history, we mention the legendary films The Splashed Sprinkler, The Arrival of a Train at Ciotat Station and the Exit of the Workers from the Lumière Plants.

Beautiful and plastic reconstruction of how the historical moment of the birth of cinematography on the Romanian territory took place is made by

Marian Țuțui in the work History of Romanian film in 7000 words:

"The first filming in Romania was made for Lumière by French optician and photographer Paul Menu (1876-1973): Royal Parade of May 10, 1897, / His Majesty the King on horseback, taking his place on the boulevard to preside over the parade. Another 16 news filmed followed within two months: the Santa's Fair, the Băneasa Hippodrome and Races, the Capșa Cafe Terrace, the Galați Floods, the Land Marine Exercises, the Danube Flotilla Vessels, etc. It is interesting that Paul Menu remained in Romania for a while and was considered a Romanian filmmaker, while his camera was purchased by Dr. Gheorghe Marinescu (1863-1938), who used it for his research in neurology, making, with the help of the operator Constantin M. Popescu, in 1898 the first scientific film in the world - Walking disorders in organic hemiplegia. "
(Țuțui 5)

We see that the documentary, in a primitive form, somewhat reduced to a kind of essentiality, quickly gains popularity regardless of the geographical territory. Besides this aspect, we notice how the role of cinema becomes very serious, being used in the first years of life even in medicine and scientific research, the new form of visual expression moving away quickly from the stigma of fairground fun, which he wore for some time.

In this context, it is essential to remember René Clair's words about the differences that marked the aesthetic approaches of the first filmmakers:

"The most elementary dichotomy of film aesthetics is between the first films of the Lumière brothers ... and Georges Méliès. Luis and Auguste Lumière had discovered cinema from the realm of photographic art. They saw in the invention a magnificent opportunity to reproduce reality, and the most remarkable films reproduced events ... These were called proto-films, simple and impactful. They didn't tell an actual story, they just reproduced a place, time, and atmosphere so efficiently that the public is looking forward to seeing the phenomenon.

Méliès, a stage magician, sensed the film's ability to process reality - to translate fantastic stories into images ... Significantly, many of Méliès' films had the words "nightmare" or "dream" in them. their titles. The dichotomy represented by the contrasting approaches of the Lumière and Méliès brothers is essential to the evolution of cinema and is repeated over the years in a variety of forms. "

(Monaco 233)

Thus, it can be seen that this side of reproduction of the "real" is noticed from the beginning by critics and filmmakers, but also by viewers, who often had quasi-visceral reactions during screenings.

The approach to copying reality as a means of aesthetic expression determines a reference to the first chapter of this paper, where we detailed that the way of representation using nature and man, especially through the technique of imitation, makes the Lumière brothers film not focus on copying natural elements but to emphasize the real space and its rendering faithfully, to produce a strong artistic impression.

The documentary appears at first in a form that we might consider today relatively childish if we were to assume an anachronism. His struggle against the gravity of the consumer area, fueled by the desire for maturation as a genre, pushed filmmakers to seek alternative ways for the language of cinema in an unknown realm. Hundreds of experiments and accidents, borrowed from other spheres of art (which I tried to sketch in the previous pages), have built over time what we call cinematic art today.

Even in the early days, when the films were composed of a single frame and were less than a minute long, the cinema was divided into two camps: those who tried to reproduce the real world and those who filmed directed scenes (Cousins and Macdonald 250-273).

The documentary, in its modern form, began with the appearance of the film Nanook from the North, made in 1922 by Robert Flaherty. It is known as the first feature-length documentary film in history. The word "documentary" was invented by John Grierson precisely to describe this film (Gray 41-48).

Although most of the scenes were directed to outline a more dramatic style, Grierson says of the film that it is a creative interpretation of reality rather than a pure form of audio-visual fiction (Duncan). The convention of a reality shaped in an artistic, creative way, begins to make its mark on how the next generations of documentary films will be made, and the observational documentary will make efforts to get rid of such a perspective.

Another film from the beginning of the documentary, The Man from Aran (1934) by Robert Flaherty, is built using narrative elements specific to the poetic mode, if we look at the way the scenes of the film will match the desired narrative and ending, instead of allowing reality to build its direction. Thus, this way of representation challenges us to question the authenticity of the documentary.

The world of Lumière films, where the representation of reality in a faithful copy is the cornerstone of aesthetics, quickly transforms into a directed world in which the natural elements, the characters, and their dramas are artificially constructed, only inspired by reality. It is observed that throughout the history of fine arts (synthesized in Chapter 1, as a necessary parallel for all subsequent considerations) this tendency to represent reality in a directed version is a common approach in all currents listed so far in this paper.

Impressed by the mastery shown by Robert Flaherty in making the documentary that paid universal homage to the author and celebrity in the eyes of film buffs, Grierson, who reviewed the film Nanook, joins the GPO Film Unit in England as a well-known exponent of the poetic-realist style, close to the documentary genre (Scott and Mansell 157-170).

Since 1933, the GPO has produced numerous documentaries, inspired by the production of the film Nanook from the North, to promote its activities. The films had many talented producers, including Basil Wright and Alberto Cavalcanti (both in the production team of the film Nightmail). These films are key works in understanding the mentality and living conditions of western Britain.

Grierson, as a production supervisor and narrator, co-directed with his fellow directors Harry Watt and Basil Wright in 1936, the documentary Nightmail, conceived in the conceptual phase as an informational film about the railway mail linking London to Edinburgh. The film follows the story of the midnight postal train, between London and Scotland, channeling our attention to several scenes: the sorting room, the loading of the train, and the inspired way of collecting correspondence from various places by catching bags at high speeds in a retractable net. The last ten minutes have as an external voice a famous poem by WH Auden, narrated rhythmically on the music of Benjamin Britten, a rhythm that imitates the sounds of the train. More than that,

The choice of scenes, the composition in the frame, the whole concept implemented poetically, in which we find movement, light, sound as leitmotifs carefully directed in the vision of the mentioned directors, are harshly commented by the critics' union, which draws attention to the fact that the author neglects political and social issues touched on by the subject in favor of a modernist approach, celebrating machinery more than the human being (Scott and Mansell 157-170).

The documentary shows us once again that the label of a neutral observer and not involved in the story is just an element of the gender-specific dichotomy. We also see how cinematic art, after less than a few decades of existence, manages to take its attention from man as a central character and can direct it on other elements, a phenomenon which, as we have seen in the aesthetics of the visual arts, is realized with the same freedom in other artistic currents (expressionism, impressionism, abstractionism, futurism, etc.).

2.2. The film of political propaganda and its relationship with the poetic mode

The film is a unique environment in which images, movement, sound are reproduced, in a natural way, drawing the evolutionary meaning of things as time passes. Unlike many other art forms, the film produces a sense of spontaneity in which the naturalness of the overall movements generates a profound impact on the human subconscious (Walter).

While the term propaganda has acquired a strongly negative connotation by associating it with its most manipulative and vile examples, propaganda in its original sense has been neutral and could refer to generally positive uses, such as the recommendations of public health, encouraging citizens to participate in the census or elections, or messages encouraging people to report crimes, for law enforcement (Gander).

The ruling class in any type of government - especially the totalitarian ones - considered the film an important tool of propaganda, of manipulating society.

On this point, it is interesting to note a few words from the work of Michael Russell:

"To return to the development of Soviet cinema, it can be said that probably the most significant effect of the Great War, the two revolutions of 1917

and the ensuing civil war was the institutional and material collapse of the tsarist film industry. The Soviet government was therefore forced to build its film industry out of almost nothing. After the February Revolution, there was an unstoppable hemorrhage of raw materials in the film industry - producers and directors fled the political and economic instability of revolutionary Russia, taking with them props, cameras, and precious films. "
(Russell 17)

In the years after the October 1917 revolution, the Soviet government sponsored the film industry to make propaganda films. The ideological tendency of Soviet cinema - its status as a form of political rhetoric rather than a purely aesthetic attempt - found a strong model in the biased approach of Vladimir Mayakovsky's poetry, which in some respects was considered (and considered itself) the bearer. unofficial word of the entire Russian left-wing vanguard of the 1920s (Russell 17-20).

The development of Russian cinema in the 1920s by filmmakers such as Dziga Vertov and Sergei Eisenstein led to considerable progress in the use of film as a propaganda tool, but at the same time, it also served to develop the universal language of cinema. Dziga Vertov, a pioneer of Russian film, proves to us in The Man with the Camera that what the audience sees is not reality, but rather a construction of reality (intellectual construction, doubled by a film construction). Reality is mediated by the subjectivity of the documentary, which is a way of representation, thus delivering to the public a particular method of deciphering that reality.

We discover this philosophy of subjectivity borrowed by the filmmakers to the poetic documentary which, using the aesthetic means developed in propaganda films, manages to advance a highly customized representation of reality. The expressive power of these elements of aesthetics has been promoted and used both in documentaries and in fiction products, such as films, commercials, or music videos.

We see how in a film from the beginnings of cinematography (1929) "from the point of view of cinematic language, the whole field of visual expressions known in cinema from filming to editing is explored: idling, zooming, animation, stop-frame, the divided screen, the blurred focus, the multiple images, all of them arranged to the full potential of the cinematographic language "(Șopterean 46). Thus, we understand that film as a medium already allowed, through the complexity of the language used, the imposition of certain directions or universally accepted perceptual/aesthetic standards.

Eisenstein's films, such as Battleship Potemkin, are seen as masterpieces of classical cinema, remaining in history as reference films for film lovers or filmmakers. The film October (1927), directed by the same author, describes the Bolshevik perspective on the revolution that culminated in the assault on the Winter Palace, offering Soviet spectators a "reconstruction" of the victory that workers and peasants dreamed of in the Battleship Potemkin. As there was no documentary material on the devastation of the palace, Eisenstein's visual recreation of the event became the source material for historians and filmmakers, giving the director further legitimacy, his success illustrating the potential of propaganda films.

Despite the occasional use of such subterfuge, Vertov hated how the public's perception of historical reality itself could be distorted by this kind of mixing of faithful techniques of documentary and news films with the fictional reconstruction of sequences. This "contamination" of historical recording by fictionalization underscores the danger that Vertov saw in any hybrid or form of cinema that tried to mix documentary mode and fictional film, as Eisenstein tried to do in his early films (Russell 13- 32).

Vertov suppressed the iconic aspect of the image in favor of its structural and symbolic aspects, to create abstract political discourses whose statements have been brought to the fore. Rather than an illusory representation of the world,

Vertov's films present a direct impression from the point of view of the organization of the universe, like a frame, an impression from which the montage can create an abstract symbolic discourse, political rhetoric to teach the viewer "decoding communist of the world "(Russell 13-32).

In most of Vertov's films, the author's interest in promoting what he considers to be the "virtues" of the Soviet state is noticeable. However, one of the important aspects of his films remains their ability to transcend the temporality of an event or social reality, consciously or not. His way of looking at and relating to the world reveals the underlying themes of the culture of all humanity in general.

With the emphasis on a totalitarian vision of a society, rigid ideology, and the cult of personality, we can say that Nazi Germany and the Soviet Union had many features in common. Both regimes also had a strong faith in propaganda to promote their political ideas.

The comparative collection of Nazi and Soviet posters, compiled by gulag.ipvnews.org, seems to indicate that the two authoritarian systems also had a similar aesthetic and approach to graphic design and not only ("Nazi And Soviet Propaganda's Shared Aesthetic "). The historical origin of Nazi propaganda can be traced back to Adolf Hitler's My Struggle, where the author wrote two chapters analyzing the importance of propaganda and its implementation (Hitler 122).

By exploiting existing stereotypes and the feelings of the German people, Nazi propaganda sought to see those it considered being enemies or unworthy of being citizens - Jews, Gypsies, homosexuals, communists, and other political dissidents, and those Germans whom they were inferior (such as people with mental or physical disabilities) - as obstacles to the creation of a strong Germany. In addition, these themes were used in the arguments for Lebensraum or living space, in close connection with the expansionist plans of Germany (Narayanaswami).

Meanwhile, Nazi directors produced extremely moving films about the suffering of the German minority in Czechoslovakia and Poland, which were crucial in creating popular support for the occupation of the southern region and the attack on Poland. Movies such as Heimkehr (Return Home) describe the longing for the motherland of ethnic Germans in Poland (Stern).

Filmed in Nazi Germany in 1941, Heimkehr shows the suppression of ethnic Germans in a small town in eastern Poland (now Ukraine) in the spring and summer of 1939. As the Polish military prepares for war, German schools are closed and looted. Minority rights are reduced or revoked. Open hostility and violence against the German people are on the rise, and the authorities are pursuing without involvement. After the outbreak of war, ethnic Germans are imprisoned in a prison where only the Wehrmacht (Nazi armed forces) save them at the last minute. The last scenes of the film shows how they are recovered and transferred back to the motherland. For today's audience, this film presents a surreal world transformed upside down, being a film produced by the Nazis that accuses ethnic persecution and a chauvinist state that treats its unwanted citizens with ruthless contempt and disrespect for the law. Many scenes and lines told by the actors, ironically, are recurring during the countless anti-Nazi films.

Thus, we discover that the world of propaganda does not stop in the last century, nor Germany. Other scenes, such as the prison where ethnic Germans were imprisoned in a crowded dark cell, have an intense, nightmare quality, and are reminiscent of Holocaust iconography for today's viewers. The reality represented in documentaries and propaganda films is far from an attempt to faithfully reproduce the real, as we have seen that has happened in other artistic currents or other cinematic genres and periods.

The documentary of the poetic mode takes over the propagandistic concept and to adapt it, as we will see in the following chapters, to the social themes of today: globalization, pollution, overwork, overpopulation, etc. Propaganda in the poetic documentary (and in other ways) keeps the same style of presenting real situations. For the emotion of social decadence (the "self-destruction" that society goes through globally) to be transmitted and received without a score, the producers of the Qatsi series stage a series of images with emotional impact in a selected intellectual order. Even if these images are, more or less, isolated phenomena, local, or present in several global areas, placed in successive order, following a certain rhythm, they generate an illusion of reality in which nothing is good., everything destroys itself. This cycle of life and death, of the struggle for survival at all costs, is resumed in later films such as Baraka and Samsara. Thus, we see the imprint that propaganda films transmit, practically, to poetic documentaries.

The 1930s and 1940s, which saw the emergence of totalitarian states and World War II, are undoubtedly the "Golden Age of Propaganda." Nazi control of the German film industry is an extreme example of the use of film as a means of psychological indoctrination of a nation, Hitler building, in 1933, the Reich Ministry for Enlightenment and Propaganda, naming the young Joseph Goebbels as a leader.

Also, many of the dramatic war films of the early 1940s in the United States were designed to generate a patriotic mood and convince viewers that the sacrifices needed to defeat the "enemy" had to be taken collectively. Despite fears that too much propaganda could diminish Hollywood's aura, reduce its target audience, and drop profits, the nation's morale has risen in part; victory attributed to America's innovative propaganda made through the film (Clayton and Black 48-50).

The education of the great masses was (and still is) accomplished by this useful tool called a documentary. This cinematic genre was not seen as a film in the true sense of the word, but as a new means of educating the population (Aufderheide 121). The purpose of propaganda is to persuade others to accept the creator's statements and to act according to the instructions (Neff. 47-50). To do this, the propagandist must convey the message in a familiar, simple, and positive way to be easily understood (Neff 47-50). More than 120 years after its creation, the film continues to resonate with and influence viewers, consolidating certain points of view that they may or may not already have.

In Benjamin Barber's analysis of war, terrorism, and its effect on democracy, Fear's Empire (2003), the author concluded that American policies after the events of 9/11 led the nation into hypocrisy, and the United States itself posed a threat to the address of democracy. The wars in Iraq and Afghanistan did not support the values and goals of democratic doctrine, the ideals of constitutional and social governance (Barber 213).

Following the 9/11 attacks, the American public was pushed by the media to empathize with the promptness shown by the US government and to support the wars that followed in Iraq and Afghanistan. In a spirit similar in many respects to the Vietnam War, filmmakers felt the need to express their feelings about the events of the film. As a reference film, we note Fahrenheit 9/11 (2004).

The film sparked debate across the country, presenting assessments of the role of the US government and its response, along with the controversy that naturally arises when recent, traumatic events arise. When Michael Moore's controversial documentary was released in the summer of 2004, it met with a large segment of the American public, people who were increasingly dissatisfied with the direction the country had taken under the Bush administration and whom they believed that in this film, for the first time, someone had given voice to the deep fears and concerns of the American population. It also did not hurt, from a commercial point of view, that the film was released during a presidential campaign, one in which the stakes never seemed higher for both ends of the political spectrum in the country.

The section dealing with the Iraq war is the most devastating part of the film, especially because

Moore can bring us emotion through the ordinary people who were directly affected by it - soldiers on the ground, amputated in the hospital and, with the greater impact, the mother of a boy killed in a helicopter crash in April 2003. Her unbearable sadness, so transparently revealed by the camera, becomes an emblem for a war that not only did not happen (as Moore points out in various ways) but was largely bought and paid for with the blood of brave women and men from the lower, disadvantaged level of society. He ends his film by confronting several politicians who voted for the war. Beyond these aspects, it is legitimate to note that the film follows a fairly classic structure of propaganda films. How the audience is led through the film through the various events or information carefully selected to present a subjective point of view is very similar to the way the working class acts or takes shape in the film October (1927). The oppression of the average person, his struggle with the corrupt system, is presented without bringing to light another perspective of events, a different point of view. But we are particularly interested in the direct connections with the poetic mode, and these stand out through the various editing techniques. Starting with the 15th minute of the movie, we have a sequence in which the diegetic sound is replaced by the sound of a church bell continued by a non-diegetic musical ambiance and a random montage with various images before, during, and after the tragic attack. The described sequence is built according to the principles of the poetic documentary, the primary goal is to arouse emotions and generate public empathy for the September 11 event. Being a recently produced film, its creators could borrow the processes developed in poetic documentaries to convey certain ideas, emotions, or information. Thus, we see that transferring cinematographic processes and means was not only made from propaganda films to the poetic mode but also in the opposite direction, showing the symbiotic relationship between these types of cinematographic products. The described sequence is built according to the principles of the poetic documentary, the primary goal is to arouse emotions and generate public empathy for the September 11 event. Being a recently produced film, its creators could borrow the processes developed in poetic documentaries to convey certain ideas, emotions, or information. Thus, we see that transferring cinematographic processes and means was not only made from propaganda films to the poetic mode but also in the opposite direction, showing the symbiotic relationship between these types of cinematographic products. The described sequence is built according to the principles of the poetic documentary, the primary goal is to arouse emotions and generate public empathy for the

September 11 event. Being a recently produced film, its creators could borrow the processes developed in poetic documentaries to convey certain ideas, emotions, or information. Thus, we see that the transfer of cinematographic processes and means was not only made from propaganda films to the poetic mode but also in the opposite direction, demonstrating the symbiotic relationship between these types of cinematographic products. Its creators were able to borrow the processes developed in poetic documentaries to convey certain ideas, emotions, or information. Thus, we see that the transfer of cinematographic processes and means was not only made from propaganda films to the poetic mode but also in the opposite direction, demonstrating the symbiotic relationship between these types of cinematographic products. its creators were able to borrow the processes developed in poetic documentaries to convey certain ideas, emotions, or information. Thus, we see that the transfer of cinematographic processes and means was not only made from propaganda films to the poetic mode but also in the opposite direction, demonstrating the symbiotic relationship between these types of cinematographic products.

The satirical way of presenting the information in Fahrenheit 9/11 (non-diegetic music and images introduced to generate parody) manages to anchor us emotionally to the subject of the film. The increased attention to the form or how the information is delivered to the public connects us directly with how the poetic mode structures the content of the afferent films.

The propaganda documentary is a documentary with a great historical impact, which manages to successfully shape the opinions of the masses of people, over time. Even though the world has changed, the level of education and information has increased (Roser and Ortiz-Ospina), its characteristics are still used today by documentary filmmakers, regardless of the documentary approach. Due to the formal nuances that the documentary can wear, it usually masks the features of propaganda, which are more difficult to detect by the general public.

2.3. The maturation of aesthetics

After the end of the Second World War, a new trend developed in contemporary culture in response to modernist confidence in an objective, scientific observation of reality as a means of progress (Sapino 13). Concepts such as objective truth and factual reality have been questioned, while others, such as relativity, plurality, and subjectivity, have emerged as the only principles by which the world could be approached (Sapino 13).

This tendency to lose the rhetoric of the discussion and to conceptually divert the emphasis from content to form is the first clear sign that the film industry has given in the sense of maturing and gaining independence from a rigid trajectory imposed by the aesthetics initially developed. The maturation of the poetic documentary depends on its external environment and the development of the universal cinematographic language, in such a way that the poetic documentary becomes a mature way, with an active influence in the evolution of cinematography.

Before talking about the documentary as a mature and independent genre, I want to quote a few illustrative and plastic words, to point out its subjective character and the force of extrapolation of its features:

"Every documentary filmmaker has his vision of the world. His political affinities, his social and economic education, all enter the filming process. From the moment he chooses a subject to the first copy from the laboratory, making a documentary film is a constant and tireless process of selection. The selections of the filmed scenes, which characters will appear on the screen, and with which lenses will be filmed, all affect the final product. The result of this long series of decisions after decisions is impossible or objective. "

(Major 4)

The reaction aroused by the movie Night Mail was the intrigue that triggered the development of technology applied in the field, and maybe even increased the reliability of the cameras. This movement gave rise to a new wave of expressive means in the cinematography of the time, leading documentary film in an area critically called direct cinema (Aitken 15). Similar in many respects to ciné-vérité (Aitken 27), direct cinema was initially characterized by filmmakers as "a desire to directly capture reality and represent it openly, questioning the relationship between reality and cinema "(Morin 7).

Direct cinema is defined as a movement started in the United States, to present social and political issues in a direct, immediate way, giving the impression that events are recorded as they happened, without the involvement of the filmmaker. The public should forget that they are watching a documentary itself. Media that have become popular in documentaries, but that make the public aware of the filming process (such as reconstructions and the external voice) have avoided allowing the camera to become reactive to the situation unfolding before it (Owen).

Mills of the Gods: Viet Nam is a documentary made in the style of direct cinema during the Vietnam War. It was filmed entirely in the field by director Beryl Fox's team for Canadian television station CBC. Fox and her crew traveled to Vietnam where they witnessed, recorded, and documented the things they saw. The film does not use archive images or narratives. All the dialogue comes directly from the mouths of the interviewees, except for the questions Fox asked the soldiers. The soldiers interviewed for the film (a few recruits and volunteers) convey a diversity of perspectives. Although many left voluntarily (to eliminate communism), others criticized the role of war in general.

Fox and her crew have been immersed in the whole Vietnam experience. Most of the film focuses on what we might call the "banalities of war": meeting friends, nightlife, meeting women, etc., but they also go out on the field to film patrols, flights.

during napalm raids, and even in forests to witness the aftermath of air warfare.

Watching this film, we can see how the film crew is involved in the historical action. If during propaganda documentaries we experience strongly defined themes such as devotion, oppression, the concept of nation, ethnicity, race, the horrors of war, we see how, in just a few decades, the documentary focuses on other topics such as nightlife or meetings with friends, even if the main action of the film remains the war, as in the aforementioned propaganda films. The film crew tries to enter the intimate universe of the characters, to discover emotions, feelings, or memories. This approach refers us to how the poetic documentary relates to an event, whether it is of some historical importance.

The development of smaller, lighter cameras, using 16mm film rollers as opposed to 35mm, which were used in feature films and documentaries until then, allowed operators to carry the devices on their shoulders and shoot in -a more spontaneous way. Among the most important representatives of this artistic movement are DA Pennebaker, The Mayles Brothers, and Fred Wiseman.

But not only the evolution of video cameras has made possible the emergence of this new trend, but also the sound recording system. Until the advent of direct cinema, the sound in the film was recorded before, in interviews, or much later in locations, with a portable studio located in a soundproof truck (Saunders 25). The captured sounds were later synchronized in the sound editing part, thus giving the film soundtrack (Saunders 39). In other cases, the soundtrack was recorded the same as in fiction films: with layers of ambient sound, archive sound effects, foley, and post-synchronized voices (Saunders 39). We conclude, therefore, as we mentioned before, that the film is the product of technological evolution and is quite dependent on it.

Modern films of the socially focused documentary genre, such as Food, Inc. (2008), Thank you for Smoking (2005), Fahrenheit 9/11 (2004) have their origins in direct cinema. The director usually has a political agenda and aims to present the events as "real", even if they are in absolute control of the editing process.

On the other hand, this current resulted from a desire to compare common opinion with reality. He tried to show how things are, outside the studio, away from the editorial control of a private company (Saunders 46). Worth noting is the very desire to test common opinion and to show the reality kept under control by sound and image (Saunders 55). This tension was at the epicenter of the current and led to its formal stylization and mythologization (Saunders 55).

At the same time that direct cinema was developed in America, a similar movement took place in France, called ciné-vérité (Introduction to Documentary, 92).

The term ciné-vérité was coined by the critic and historian Georges Sadoul, who translated Vertov's Kino-Pravda as "cine-vérité" in the History of Cinema in 1948 (Mamber 68).

Ciné-Vérité is a minimalist style of making a film, which conveys the impression that the viewer receives the raw image of what is happening in front of the camera, without the fireworks usually included in the filming process, favoring hand-held filming, natural lighting, places real filming. Invented by Jean Rouch and other pioneers such as Robert Drew, Robert Flaherty, Richard Leacock, etc., in the 1960s, it quickly acquired the important status of a significant current in documentary film (Chang). The procedures listed above such as filming in natural light (or using only existing light sources), on the shoulder, etc., are also found in the case of the poetic mode, in almost all films included in this category.

It is important to remember that this way of representing reality does not try to sell us an illusion of faithful representation, nor to deceive us about the status quo. His entire attention falls on the subjective experience that the viewer must live when watching. The same purpose was used by

Rouch during the making of his documentaries even if they are not part of the category of the poetic documentary.

We see that just as propaganda documentaries or fiction films make their mark on the aesthetics of the poetic way, so do ciné-vérité documentaries have a say in the same question of influence.

Jean Rouch's activity in Africa for over 60 years has been characterized, above all, by his desire to make cinema a scientific tool in the service of cultural anthropology. Discovering surrealism at the age of 20, many of his films are built along the fine line between fiction and documentary, the author creating a new style: ethnonational ("Glossary Of Rouchian Terms").

Among his popular films is Les Maîtres Fous (1955), a film whose subject is the Hauka movement. According to some anthropologists, this movement was a form of resistance that began in Niger but quickly spread to other parts of the world. It's about a religious form that combines elements of traditional African religions with influences from the colonizers, in an extremely interesting synthesis. In Jean Rouch's film, a ritual is a meticulously documented hack, including shocking scenes, such as dipping your hand in hot water or ritually eating dog meat.

Rouch's films largely belonged to the cine-vérité school, as we can see from a simple analysis. His best-known film, one of the central works of the Nouvelle Vague (New Wave), is Chronique d'été (1961), which was filmed in the company of sociologist Edgar Morin and portrays the social life of contemporary France. However, the techniques used in cine-vérité have also been borrowed by dramatic film directors, such as Ken Loach, who used the term docudrama to describe the hybrid genre born of the shock of the meeting of the two genres. Together with Jean-Michel Arnold, he founded the Cinéma du Réel International Documentary Film Festival at the Pompidou Center in Paris in 1978,

Film critics have defined the major difference between these two genres as the author's direct involvement in the narrative. If in ciné-vérité the presence of the author in front of the camera was necessary to give high veracity to the subject, indirect cinema was avoided (Nam). All these particularities apply to classify the mentioned genera and to observe the similarities and differences between them. The poetic mode, however, aims at a multitude of aspects that are built on the elements of language and directorial approach, but the conceptualization and intellectualization of the production process made the poetic documentary go beyond the limits of the subject, which, despite the democratization undertaken by the directors of direct cinema and ciné-vérité, he could not or did not want to be treated. Specifically, the subjective approach of the subject could be, along the way, loaded with fictional elements that build the directorial concept in a form closer to the main aim of the current (that of inducing the public a feeling as close as possible to direct involvement in the subject) despite the restrictions imposed by the criteria of representation of reality.

In comparison, direct cinema and ciné-vérité seek to discover the truth in two different ways. The first hopes to reveal the truth by the camera's observation of events and subjects; the latter uses every means (but without the involvement of the elements of fiction) to seek the truth and involves an internal process that is gradually revealed (Nam).

In trying to understand the establishment of observation as the only method of manifesting a documentary with a capacity to achieve a genuine reproduction of life, it is important to establish the source of this statement. If we consider the fact that the camera is a recording device, then the act of filming becomes eminently scientific through the use of technology to investigate the phenomena of life, social or historical (Renov 92).

This way of directly observing phenomena to document, often, the aesthetic and emotional capacities of reality is also how Stan Brakhage (for example) made most of his poetic documentaries.

The world of emotions and sensory reactions becomes the epicenter of his films, proving once again that the reality represented throughout our history by all artistic precedents can be seen and isolated, only from the perspective of a small number of criteria. Isolating the subject from a wide universe of subjects and using particular procedures in its representation is the strategy that documentary filmmakers have in this period of genre maturation.

2.4. Modern documentaries and the issue of contemporary aesthetics

As modern critics seem to suggest, the aesthetics of contemporary documentary is an attempt to "beautify" the content of films, making it acceptable to an audience accustomed to multiplex entertainment (Owen 4).

Over time, the viewer became more interested not in what he saw, but in how the perception was orchestrated. Probably this tendency is also maintained by the finite number of realities that can be represented concerning our spatial dimensions and to the relationship we maintain with space. The intention of the creator is defined by the space between the seen object and the viewer, by eliminating the previous separation between subject and object. This emancipation was not possible until the evolution of the technique that allowed the capitalization of perception in a dynamic way. But in a set of limited spatial elements, filmed and re-filmed by hundreds of thousands of creators, the only ways to produce new content have come to depend exclusively on how the subject is approached.

The successive appearance of photography, cinema, television, new media, through the amounts of information and their increasingly complex structuring, allowed the progressive development of new aesthetic and ontological paradigms.

Reality is transposed by modern means into hyperreality, and the gap between the real presence and the virtual presence is deepening day by day. The recorded image becomes a way of communicating and transmitting information, whose functionality begins to take precedence over aesthetics. Preserving a credible concept is done in the same way as in the aesthetics of realism that we talked about in Chapter 1. Reality becomes a lever to the authentic, to the palpable, but at the same time reality must be simulated by sensory stimuli, a process made with symbols and formal elements, which we talked about in the previous pages.

The way documentaries were exposed changed radically, 20 years later, after the emergence of the ciné-vérité trend in the 1960s, in which the use of portable cameras and easy-to-handle sound equipment allowed for an intimate relationship between the director and subject (Klotman and Cutler 34). The moving, permeable boundary between documentary and narrative film emerges from the classic area of the film as a historical document or reflection of a form of reality as can be seen in Marlon Riggs' Tongues Untied (1989) and Black is ... Black is not (1995), which mixes expressive, poetic, rhetorical elements and emphasizes subjectivities, rather than historical truths (Klotman and Cutler 71).

One of the fundamental problems facing almost any modern documentary, regardless of the size and distribution of the budget, is that in a fragmented media system, with a variety of content choices, most consumers of audiovisual material who have no interest in political issues or general culture considers it very easy to avoid this kind of film (Nisbet 1-2).

Even the so-called blockbuster documentaries fall victim to the forces of selectivity. For example, following the 2004 presidential election, a Pew poll indicated that 31% of American adults reported seeing a political documentary in the last year related to the campaign or candidates (Nisbet 1-2).

I would like to summarize, at this moment, some statistical data on the audience of documentary films, to be aware of their importance in the media market and where exactly the poetic documentary is located.

In the study published in September 2014 by Maria De Rosa and Marilyn Burgess, entitled Learning from Documentary Audiences: A Market Research Study, 50,000 questionnaires were sent centralizing a total of 3,271 responses across Canada.

When asked how viewers discover documentaries, they supported various methods such as reviews, recommendations from friends, etc. But only 7% of those interviewed said they could find documentation easily, and 62% answered that they see documentaries online because they have no other chance to see them.

The classic satellite or fiber optic distribution network remains a relatively closed circuit for trend waves that appear overnight and for amateur documentaries.

We also have a growing trend of audience. 68% of those who responded to the study said that they watch more documentaries today than three years ago, while only 4% watch less. Despite these trends, the audience of television channels specific to the documentary film format - such as Discovery, National Geographic, or History - is kept far below the numbers of entertainment stations, news or fiction films.

In Romania, according to the paginademedia.ro website, the audience for the whole month of January 2018 was, in thousands of people, the following: Pro TV 1712, Kanal D 1195, Pro Cinema 119, Paramount 51, National Geographic 18, Discovery 21, History 21. In a chart presented by statista.com, we see the preferences of viewers of television stations in the United States. Comparing the number of viewers of Discovery or History stations in the USA with the number of viewers of news or entertainment, we notice that it is even 8 times smaller. in Romania even more than 90 times smaller.

Another chart on statista.com made for October 2017, about the American public, shows the percentage of viewers depending on the type of program. Thus, we can easily see that although the number of viewers or interest in documentaries increases from year to year, this progress remains at a limited level. Only 1% of all viewers chose to watch a television channel dedicated to the documentary genre.

Looking at things from the perspective of cinemas we can follow the success of some documentaries. We talked earlier about the movie Fahrenheit 9/11 (2004) and it is elementary to remember its success. According to the website imdb.com, the film had grossed a total of $ 222,446,320 by January 2005, starting with an estimated budget of $ 6,000,000. Also, one of the most successful poetic documentaries remains The Emperor's Way (2005), with an estimated budget of $ 8,000,000.

(imdb.com) and $ 127,392,693. We must not ignore, however, that much of the success of these examples is due to the important awards received. According to the boxofficemojo.com website, only 28 documentaries of all time managed to raise more than 10 million dollars in cinemas, while more than

300 fiction films that were made in 3D format alone had more than 10 revenues. millions of dollars.

Certainly, this analysis cannot summarize a correct and clear picture of global trends in viewing documentaries, but they can help us to see that the documentary market remains dedicated to a growing audience, but restricted, despite the success of several films.

Although documentaries are much more financially viable, with the growing popularity of the genre and the advent of DVDs, funding for documentary film production remains an area at least problematic (Keenlyside). In the last decade, the biggest funding opportunities have appeared on the media market, forcing filmmakers to make films adapted to the tastes and influences of the broadcasting area (Keenlyside).

Modern documentaries intertwine with certain forms of television materials, with the development of the Reality Television area, which relies on the credible side of the documentary but exaggerates through the fiction and falsity of the topics presented. Modern and light video cameras, whose filmed content can be edited in special programs on personal computers, have come like a spring in the desert, for documentary filmmakers (Sfetcu 7). One of the first films to take advantage of this opportunity was Voices of Iraq, directed by Martin Kunert and Eric Manes (Stevens). During the war,

150 DV cameras were used by Iraqis to film, and these materials were later used to make the film (Stevens).

Historical documents such as The Years of American Civil Rights by Henry Hampton, 4 Little Girls by Spike Lee, and the Civil War by Ken Burns, awarded by UNESCO as an independent film about slavery, expressed not only a distinct voice but also a perspective and a point of view. see (Wood). Some films, such as The Thin Blue Line by Errol Morris, incorporated stylized reconstructions, and Roger & Me, by Michael Moore, put much more interpretive control in the hands of the director (Wood).

In recent years, the progressive spread of accessible technologies, along with public frustration with traditional concepts, pressure from an information-hungry audience, and the work of notable (often controversial) directors such as Errol Morris or Michael Moore, have led the documentary to the mainstream world. (Sapino 2).

The documentary proved to be subversive for its ability to reinvent itself when cultural changes occur, changes that took place in the contemporary era, thus calling into question its very existence, and for its ability to push its limits to fiction. , to find new ways of not representing "reality", but the problematic plurality of its perceptions (Sapino 13).

At a careful and thorough analysis, undertaken in a broad comparative perspective, we discover these aesthetic properties as part of a universal circuit. The path of the documentary seems to be inspired by the aesthetic course of the Italian Renaissance (see Chapter 1), influenced by the strong changes in technological, historical, political, social, cultural, etc.

We are already seeing movements towards different modes of production and exposure. Websites such as Documentary.org demonstrate that filmmakers can now bypass traditional film and television production environments to satisfy an immediate global audience, but also to contribute more to shaping the tastes and availability of diverse audience categories. Today's commercial methodology and even cinematic exposure seem to be about to become key moments in a retrospective history (Sapino 16).

New Media or Web-Documentary is a new form of audiovisual expression characterized by the exclusivity of consumption in the area of online platforms and mobile applications. Supported by platforms built exclusively for audiovisual materials specially prepared for them, the New Media Documentary is developed by combining several interactive means that technology offers.

As the definition of the documentary tells us, the documentary is the exploration of as yet undiscovered universes, and through these modern means, the diversity of methods increases exponentially. The potential of modern communication platforms and methods is virtually limitless. It all depends on the creativity and solutions that developers discover.

Another important feature is the interactivity or the ability of the platform to offer the public the opportunity to interact with the materials, to make choices, to communicate with other users, to live unique experiences, and, at the same time, to be able to stop actions or follow another course of stories between several possible.

The number of these platforms increases from year to year, developing new audiovisual paradigms. The future looks promising for filmmakers, researchers, and developers of these alternative ways of audiovisual communication, offering users the tools to explore and know the surrounding phenomena, characterized by opportunities to assimilate information extremely fast and pleasant. The documentary thus opens its doors to a new era of communication. Technology is easily becoming one engine that engages the public in this complex mechanism of the media industry and on which the very existence and evolution of poetic documentary depend.

3. Aesthetics and genres of documentary film

This chapter aims to point out, through thorough research, the genres, subgenres, as well as the influences or differences between the narrative structures in documentaries. This journey of research will begin with the work of pioneers in the field such as Paul Rotha, Bill Nichols, or Ian Aitken.

Documentary modes are a system by which films can be classified into one of many subdivisions of the genre. However, this approach has not remained uncritical. Tony de Bromhead opposes the ways as they were circumscribed by Nichols, arguing that the core of the documentary story lies in the emotional response, and the source of empathy and distinction should be sought in narrative structures that serve as an interpolation between world and self, as opposed to of Nichols's objective concerns (Bromhead 21).

Bromhead draws attention to the difficulty of classifying hybrid documentaries according to the ways and criteria of classification presented by Nichols in his works, giving us an example of the Fourth Industrial Revolution (2016), directed by Marta Chierego. The film is presented in the form of a montage of poetic images and cut-outs of interviews on a single major theme. There are elements of the exhibition mode in the film, many of the frames being rendered over the construction of an aim external voice. But after a few images, the external voice is attributed to a character we see continuing the speech. This emphasizes the position of the actors as subjects of the film and strengthens their subjectivity, which contradicts the conventional exhibition-style: to make the narrator appear as if what he is saying is pure truth, aim. The film also features sequences from the poetic mode described by Nichols, especially in terms of visual montages reminiscent of the 1982 film Koyaanisqatsi. Unlike most films of the poetic mode, however, the Fourth Industrial Revolution contains a lot of coherent, spoken narratives that act towards a central and unambiguous argument, rather than leaving it open for interpretation. The film could be better classified according to Bromhead's episodic model, in which the meaning is produced by the juxtaposition of situations around the dominant theme of the film. Unlike most films of the poetic mode, however, The Fourth Industrial Revolution contains a lot of coherent, spoken narratives that act towards a central and unambiguous argument, rather than leaving it open for interpretation. The film could be better classified according to Bromhead's episodic mode, in which the meaning is produced by the juxtaposition of situations around the dominant theme of the film. Unlike most films of the poetic mode, however, The Fourth Industrial Revolution contains a lot of coherent, spoken narratives that act towards a central and unambiguous argument, rather than leaving it open for interpretation. The film could be better classified according to Bromhead's episodic mode, in which the meaning is produced by the juxtaposition of situations around the dominant theme of the film.

I will not insist on the criticisms of Nichols' theory, because they are built around the exceptions to the fundamental rules; concretely, they revolve around hybrid documentaries that cannot be classified or described entirely in the ways developed by Nichols. Therefore, these hybrid documentaries must be structured and classified according to additional sets of rules and criteria that can follow the same reasoning of the narrative structure or can be characterized using the criterion of emotional response, as Bromhead suggests. Basically, besides Nichols' theory (developed in 1991 and republished in 2010 under the title Introduction to Documentary), there should be secondary, hybrid modes with their own set of rules to cover these theoretical gaps.

Sandra Gaudenzi tried to develop such a model regarding the viewer's interaction with the documentary which we will discuss in Chapter 5.

But let's see rather here what the conceptual scheme developed by the American theorist Bill Nichols looks like, which seeks to distinguish certain features and conventions of different styles of documentary film. Nichols identifies six different documentary modes in his scheme: poetic, expository, observational, participatory, reflective, and performative (Introduction to Documentary, 99). While Nichols' discussion of modes progresses chronologically with the order in which they appear, in practice, the documentary often returns to themes and features from previous modes. Therefore, it is inaccurate to think of ways as historical punctuation marks in the evolution towards a universally accepted documentary style (Introduction to Documentary, 99).

I would like to argue the choice of Nichols citation dominantly throughout this chapter, emphasizing that Bill Nichols, through his works, achieves the broadest and most well-structured classification of the documentary film, a classification cited, followed, completed by most researchers in the field.

To better understand this aspect, I will briefly present a series of specialized works that quote and develop Nichols' ideas. One of the eloquent examples is the book entitled Documenting the Documentary: Close Readings of Documentary (1998), where Nichols' vision of the poetic features identified in documentaries is carefully followed and emphasized throughout several chapters.

Also, in the book Topics in Audiovisual Translation (2004), the same Nichols is quoted several times in the chapter Myths About Documentary Translation, which points out the versatility of how the documentary can be researched.

John Corner on page 260 of Performing the Real: Documentary Diversions tells us in parentheses that "Bill Nichols' work - Representing Reality: Issues and Concepts in Documentary (1991) - is the major text for the development of the United States and an essential reference for all work on this subject "(Corner, 260).

Several other authors such as Michael Renov in Theorizing Documentary (1993), Carl Plantinga in "What a Documentary Is After All" (2005), or Annabelle Honess Roe in Animated Documentary (2013) brings to our attention aspects of his classifications.

This classification of Nichols not only allows us to study poetic documentary film methodologically, following the way it evolves, in close connection with research methods and with methods developed and applied by other researchers in the field but also offers us multiple possibilities to approach the content through methodological levers presented in his works.

Returning to the subject, we notice that documentarians, choosing more and more often customized topics on various topics less known to the general public, tend to get involved in interpreting the nature of events, altering their natural course, thus resulting in form exploitation of the public. He tends to take the film as absolute truth, without a thorough investigation of the problem. The study of the aesthetics of documentary film, of the forms and techniques of imaginative creativity, of the pleasures and satisfactions it generates, has not been - surprisingly - strongly targeted by researchers. They were not intrigued by the way documentaries to construct and project their knowledge, interpretation, and probable use by viewers (Austin and de Jong 20).

Also in Bill Nichols' book, Introduction to Documentary, we discover a form of classification of documentaries according to the leitmotifs present in editing, image, sound, and direction, as well as according to the narrative structure. The author wants to draw attention to the similarities between different documentaries, actively involving us - as spectators - in their discovery.

Beyond the mentioned aspects, we will direct our attention in a structured way, in the following, on the aspects that I consider relevant in terms of the evolution of the aesthetics of the poetic documentary seen through the prism of the existing documentary modes.

3.1. The origin and evolution of poetic documentaries

We will begin our analysis with a brief introduction to the aesthetics of poetic documentaries to have a clear starting point to write the comparative study whose realization we have proposed as the primary purpose of this doctoral thesis. This brief introduction will be extrapolated and detailed, especially during the next chapter where we will consider only the aspects and features specific to the poetic mode.

Following the same pattern as avant-garde films, poetic documentaries first appeared in the 1920s, being a reaction against visual content and grammar, which were already beginning to be applied more and more mechanically in the construction of fiction films. They implement a visual asymmetry (in terms of contrasts between successive images), as I will try to show in Chapters 4 and 5, destroying the cliché of organizing images according to classical models, in terms of time and space. The characters, built in an almost heroic form until then, in fiction films, become similar entities to ordinary people in society. The disturbance of the Spatio-temporal coherence can be seen as the key elements of the modernist era, manifested in the texture of these films.

The first documentary filmmakers, enthusiastic about Soviet editing theory and Impressionist cinematography, mastered these techniques in making documentaries to create what Nichols later called the poetic mode. The pioneer of the documentary, Vertov, made an excellent description of the poetic mode even though it was not yet defined as such and circumscribed from a theoretical point of view: "Kinochestvo is the art of organizing the movements of objects in space as rhythmic harmony, in harmony with the properties of the material and the internal rhythm of each object "(Vertov and Michelson 7). This internal rhythm, which Vertov talks about, is the main feature concerning the functional mechanism of the concept.

The poetic mode is manifested by a strongly subjectivized interpretation of the content chosen to be treated in the documentary. The traditional narrative subject is abandoned: individual characters and events remain undeveloped in favor of constructing free states or forms of subjectivity. This is remarkable in the editing of poetic documentaries, in which the classical continuity of the narrative thread does not exist. Rather, poetic editing explores "associations and patterns that involve temporal rhythms and spatial juxtapositions" (Introduction to Documentary, 44).

The subject is built around poetic audio-visual associations. The films avoid following a specific story or conventional narrative logic, use stylistic figures similar to poetry, such as metaphor, comparison, and disjunction, but also a similar structuring of the material. This is why the module is called poetic.

One of the most famous films, framed in the poetic mode, is the film made by Joris Ivens, entitled Regen (1929). Regen is the paradigmatic example of the poetic mode, consisting of images that are not in a clear connection but are linked together to render an autumn rain in Amsterdam. Because the poetic mode illustrates such subjective impressions with little or no narrative content, it is often perceived as avant-garde, and modern documentaries, such as Samsara by Ron Fricke, have continued the same formal pattern (Introduction to Documentary, 33).

The French philosopher Gilles Deleuze (in his book on cinema, Cinema 1. The image-movement) offers a wonderful description of this film in which he claims that the film is no longer a representation of rain, but tries to give the viewer the pure feeling of "quality" of rain, called "qualification".

The documentary is, however, very similar to the popular film Symphony City, which we cannot overlook. The City's symphonies, such as those created by Ruttman, Cavalcanti, and Vertov, obviously vary in the cities presented, but also in the treatment of subjects and the prominence of the director's voice in structure: Ruttman's film turned

Berlin into the main character, while Vertov's film it is extremely reflective (MacDonald 87).

Initially, Joris Ivens' cinematographic activity focused on technique, his relatives saying that the director relied, in particular, on the relevance of conceptual expressiveness, outstanding performance in the aforementioned film, providing impressive images and a series of characters, but no precise information about them.

Joris Ivens lived between 1898-1989 and during this time he created thirteen noteworthy documentaries, films whose interdependence and revolutionary vision shaped the trajectory of documentary film. Throughout his career, Ivens has made art films, commercial films, political, war, and anti-war documentaries. His final film, The Story of the Wind (1988), is a creation with a pronounced autobiographical note, representing the contemplation of the gap between realism and fantasy.

Another poetic film, important to mention is Sans Soleil (1982), directed by French director Chris Marker. Sans Soleil is a meditation on human nature, presenting the inability of organic memory to remember the context and nuances of events. Thus, the perception of personal and global history is dramatically affected. This experimental essay is a composition of thoughts, images, and scenes, especially from Japan and Guinea-Bissau, two extreme poles of survival.

These directors, avant-garde through their cinematographic works, show us the way to a different aesthetic: an aesthetic of emotions, of subtle feelings on a personal level, which must be experienced while watching the cinematographic product. It gives us the time to reflect on these emotions through the techniques we use. We are trapped in a space where we experience a fragment of real-life or a description of what a person's real-life experience would mean.

3.2. The transition to exhibition documentaries

John Grierson explains moving away from the poetic documentary claiming that directors "were caught up in social propaganda ... We came to the social problems of the world and we deviated from the poetic line" (Sussex and Grierson 24). The expository mode differs directly from the poetic mode in terms of visual practice and narrative structuring mode, under the emphasis on rhetorical content and its purposes of disseminating information or convincing the public (Sussex and Grierson 24).

Narration is an important feature of the expository mode. If in the poetic mode the directorial vision focused on the visual-aesthetic interpretation of a subject, the exhibition mode collects images that have the role of strengthening the spoken narrative. This mode is addressed directly to the viewer, often in the form of an authorial commentary, using authoritative voices or tones, proposing a solid and well-argued point of view.

Based on high-class rhetoric, the mentioned films try, through their imposing style, to convince the viewer of the veracity of the assumptions exposed to the analysis. The comment sounds "objective" and omniscient, getting a serious note. Images are often not extremely important, their existence is justified, in particular, by the strengthening of the argument proposed by the premise of the external narrative voice.

Rhetoric constantly pressures us to read images in a certain way, restricting our freedom to see ourselves as spectators, the essence of the phenomena exposed. This category includes most science and nature documentaries made by the BBC, Discovery, and other mainstream television networks.

Probably the most familiar example of this type of relationship between the external voice and the image, which we talked about in the previous chapter, is Night Mail (1936), one of the first documentaries:

"Although the external voice has an informative character, its lyrical form seems to have, in fact, a propagandistic intention to encourage the working class and emphasize its importance at a time when an industrial war is imminent. This, to some extent, strengthens Nichols' idea of accepting the existence of a "direct relationship between images and the external voice."

("Expository Mode")

As reference author films we have Ways Of Seeing (1972) made, in three parts, by John Berger and broadcast by the BBC. The film illustrates the content of the book of the same name, content built by a group of authors represented by Berger, Sven Blomberg, Chris Fox, and Richard Hollis. It is a collection of essays that focuses mainly on representations of women in commercials and oil paintings. The first part of the television series reflects on the ideas highlighted by Walter Benjamin in his book, The Work of Art in the Age of Mechanical Reproduction (2015), arguing that by reproducing the context in which a work of art was created in a period before contemporaneity, art consumers and beauticians degrade the true artistic vision, through the opinions and criticisms brought to the work. In my opinion, one of the properties of the artistic product is its proximity or distance from the public, depending on the set of values to which it refers at the time of its consumption and the issuance of critical opinions. Thus, it is essential that the artistic product (in our case the documentary film) not only remain an element projected or suspended on a wall but be integrated as part of the reality from which it detached.

The second film debates the female nude from a historical, pictorial perspective. Berger states that only twenty or thirty ancient masters describe the woman from a purely platonic perspective following her true naturalness. The others adhering to this theme rather satisfy the idolatry of their vision about woman, or out of erotic hedonism. These intimate desires and intrusions of the expository mode show us its connection with the poetic mode, where the intimate perspective of the subject remains the fundamental element in representation.

The third part refers to the use of oil paint to describe or reflecting the condition of the persons who commissioned the work of art. In the fourth program in which the subject focuses on advertising, the author claims color photography has taken on the role of oil paint, although the context is reversed. The symbols, represented in advertising, which took the place of painters' models, are stereotypes idealized by the consumer market, substitutes for the natural reality described in the paintings of the great masters.

Currently, the exhibition mode is mainly associated with documentaries about nature, such as The Blue Planet. Here, David Attenborough's voice explains the evolution, environment, and habits of ocean life ("Expository Mode"). Assuming that Bill Nichols is right about the close relationship between images and voice, perhaps the documentary builds a preferred meaning because the audience is not encouraged to investigate images and narration independently ("Expository Mode").

Although this, in theory, distorts reality, it must be taken into account that the intentions of the exhibition mode are educational and, therefore, research must have been carried out to legitimately present a certain vision, especially with science-oriented documentaries such as would be The Blue Planet ("Expository Mode").

However, in the same way, that the poetic mode directs the audience to a certain conclusion through visual means and poetic "manipulation", the expository mode conquers by presenting a reality constructed from verbal domination, leading the audience in the process of complex and detailed narrative understanding of exhibition documentaries ("Expository Mode").

Exposure codes and conventions according to Nichols:
- Interviews
- External voice
- Archive of images and movies
- The word is more important than the image - the image is there to support the argument
- Editorial editing
- The music
- It addresses the viewer directly
- It is possible to view raw images
- Graphics and illustrative animation
- Dramatic reconstruction
- subtitles

- The impression of objectivity or well-supported argument
- Good for transmitting information or mobilizing support.

    (Introduction to Documentary, 107-109)

With high popularity, this way of documentary imposes itself, for the time being, in most television programs or cinemas through the degree of direct addressing, the simplicity of the narrative structure, and the familiarity of the concept. His relationship with other modes of documentary, in particular with poetic documentary, is probably centered on the topics addressed, but not on the language tools used in the construction of the film product.

3.3. The poetic, the observational, and the participatory

Each style or documentary mode has its distinctive features, but most documents are not built exclusively in one certain way but combine more than one style. That is why it is essential in research to constantly look at these ways of documenting through the method of comparison.

The observational mode developed during the flowering of documentaries tends to return to the Vertovian ideal of truth, as shown by the analysis of specialized documents made during this paper and the analysis of the evolution of technology in the 60s. they allowed documentarians to leave the anchor point that the tripod represented for a long time. Unlike the subjective content of poetic documentaries or the rhetorical insistence of expository documentaries, observational documentaries tend to simply observe a phenomenon that allows viewers to conclude on their facts about the events or people presented to them.

Filmmakers can enter directly into the middle of situations, without altering events due to technological limitations. Pure observational documentaries are presented in the form of fragments of recorded reality that completely lack music, interviews, directed scenography, and narration. The equipment needed to make a documentary could be reduced to just two people - one to operate the camera and the other to record the sound.

The Hospital (Frederick Wiseman, 1970) was one of the first observational documentaries that, without a doubt, managed to draw a relatively authentic representation of reality. The development of the camera's capabilities, as mentioned earlier, allowed filmmakers to track hospital events as they unfolded, recreating a sense of time, speed, and timeline that had a very high impact on the audience (Observational Mode "). Also, filmmakers were no longer restricted by the space of a film set and were able to record in private areas, such as operating theaters, offering the public fresh and interesting scenes to study ("Observational Mode").

The less invasive camera also means that subjects can continue their normal lives (Introduction to Documentary, 34), thus suggesting that observational documentaries could transpose an accurate representation of reality ("Observational Mode"). For example, at doctor-patient consultations in the hospital, small rooms allowed subjects to ignore the fact that they were filmed, most of the time. However, even if the cameras were smaller, this did not make them invisible; therefore, it cannot be guaranteed that the actions presented are, in any event, true copies of what would normally happen in the absence of the film crew and the equipment used ("Observational Mode").

An entire generation of documentarians have embraced the new observational style and made extensive use of the advantages of technological advances. The most controversial aspect of realistic cinema resulted from the fact that the camera could transpose reality directly, including penetrating the social area and at the same time revealing profound truths about man and the invisible nature.

An American Family, the film edited in a twelve-part series, in Craig Gilbert's vision, broadcast on public television in 1973, tried to capture the normal life of a modest family, revealing the ordinary realities of the middle class, a part integral part of American society. In this observational documentary, the presence of the camera was integrated so as not to affect the characters to a significant level, and if it did, the filmmakers chose only those moments when we discover the person hidden behind the social facade. The filming mode often focused on subjective angles, hand-held footage (without stabilization) shows us how the observational documentary manages to capture emotions from the usual intimacy of a character.

Perhaps the most extreme example of this approach was Portrait of Jason (Shirley Clarke, 1967), a film that consists entirely of a series of close-ups with a failed actor who, due to a failure fueled by alcohol, marijuana, and the cause of questions asked from behind the camera gives up his social, intellectual curtain, sinking into self-pity. The constant use of the foreground during the film and the direct addressing of the spectator (the character looking in the room) are techniques used during poetic documentaries like Baraka or Samsara, where we often see characters standing nailed and looking directly into the room in the foreground, but very rarely they talk to us, their presence being a conceptual, symbolic one.

An important figure in American documentary film, Frederick Wiseman, began the effort to make an extraordinary series of award-winning films during the direct cinema movement of the 1960s. Over three decades, he produced more than thirty feature-length documentaries. -film and won numerous awards.

Unlike films made with astronomical budgets by his more famous contemporaries (Richard Leacock, DA Pennebaker, and the Maysles brothers), Wiseman's films focus less on individuals as individuals and more on institutions of various kinds, from those focused on individual buildings (High School, 1968) to international ones (Sinai Field Mission, 1978), and from institutions established and maintained by the government (Juvenile Court,

1973) to the least tangible, organized by ideological principles and culture of that time (Model, 1980).

As a former lawyer, Wiseman captures American life more fully than any other documentary filmmaker, and taken together, his documentaries are the opposite of the concept of life in contemporary America.

Following these short film analyzes, we see how the observational documentary approaches the documentary of the poetic mode through its intrusion into the intimate-social life. If in the poetic documentary we follow mainly the emotions of the characters or the emotions and sensations transmitted by certain situations, in the observational documentary the intimate life is not presented to us with the central purpose of generating emotions. The main purpose is to know and understand the intimacy of some characters or social phenomena. Therefore, the intrusion in the observational documentary is carried out in a controlled way, trying to keep the objectivity of the observation act.

The big problem of one of the best know, as we discussed in the previous chapters and we will discuss during the paper, the representation of reality. Many of the sequences of observational documentaries are presented in the form of fragments of reality, the author trying to sell us the illusion of an unaltered reality. We have a series of observational films where several aspects denounce the level of directorial intervention: the scenographic elements were carefully chosen, the lighting mode is premeditated, placing the cameras expect the movement of the characters on stage, and the sound recording is made only from certain directions. Let's not get it wrong, in the poetic documentary the director intervenes from all these points of view in a more authoritarian form, but he does not hide his intervention, but he fully assumes it. In the observational documentaries, the assumption of the directorial intervention in the aim's alteration reality does not exist. The pressure exerted by this way of documenting on the public is high. Our expectations, as spectators, are deceived by the production team just like in a propaganda documentary. The producers know the subject very well, and through authoritarian control, they impose a scenario. Let's not forget the case of Nanook in the North where the entire film is directed, sequence by sequence, to render a representation similar to the reality observed by Flaherty in his expeditions. The pressure exerted by this way of documenting on the public is high. Our expectations, as spectators, are deceived by the production team just like in a propaganda documentary. The producers know the subject very well and through authoritarian control; they impose a scenario. Let's not forget the case of Nanook in the

North where the entire film is directed, sequence by sequence, to render a representation similar to the reality observed by Flaherty in his expeditions. The pressure exerted by this way of documenting on the public is high. Our expectations, as spectators, are deceived by the production team just like in a propaganda documentary. The producers know the subject very well, and through authoritarian control, they impose a scenario. Let's not forget the case of Nanook in the North where the entire film is directed, sequence by sequence, to render a representation similar to the reality observed by Flaherty in his expeditions.

If in most films such as the poetic, performative, or reflective mode the control of the subject and the way these films will look at the end is limited, in observational documentaries the control is authoritarian, similar to that of expository documentaries.

To better illustrate this, I will provide some concrete examples. In the film entitled This is (2001), by Thomas Ciulei, director of several observational documentaries, we have a series of sequences in which the dialogue of the characters, but also their actions, are carefully directed by the production team. In the 12th minute, for example, the two spouses return to the household yard for dinner. The characters enter the courtyard simultaneously, while the camera anticipates their every move: the order of entry, each on which trajectory it moves, what decorative objects come into contact, the order of entry into the house, arranging the decorative objects so that the scene it can be filmed without technical errors, continuously, without using multiple cameras from multiple angles. Not only was such a scene previously prepared in terms of the lights, the scenographic elements, and the movement and action of the characters, but they were most likely made.

Another simple example can be given from the film Constantin and Elena (2009), made by Andrei Dăscalescu. From the first sequences, we notice two characters, a man and a woman, in a rural household. Through a succession of fixed plans, the author presents us both their dialogue and their social interaction, as well as the "road" that the meat travels from the smoking room in the yard to the attic of the house. All this action, of moving and storing food, is directed and edited in a way that suggests a temporal fluency. The characters move from one space to another simulating a constant movement in time and space. But such an action could be done only by the previous positioning of the cameras in all the chosen places, the protagonists being carefully directed on the initially established route, or the scene took place being filmed with a single camera, this being repositioned according to the evolution of the action on the established route. In both situations, the director's intervention regarding the way of carrying out the "observed" action transforms the reality watched in a sequence similar to those in fiction films.

Such directions are not far below the level of involvement and direction in fiction films, reaffirming the hypocrisy of the documentary genre. The big problem does not result from the fact that they present events in an altered way, but because they claim to provide a faithful representation of reality.

The observational documentary remains a different mode of documentary expression than poetic documentary, but it helps us to understand, as documentarians, how you can relate to reality, the differences, and the connections between them. We see how the observational meets the poetic through the elements of stage direction, by presenting intimate subjects or using visual symbols, but it also moves away from it by the neutral positioning of the camera, the lack of fictional, conceptual stories, or experimental passages.

We discussed the differences and connections between the first two ways presented in the title, but we left the participle to describe more systematically the plasticity of the aesthetics that we want to describe as accurately as possible in this research.

Participatory documentaries start from the premise that a film cannot be made without intervention and, implicitly, an alteration, to a certain extent, of the events captured by the camera. What is tried through this category of films is an anthropological imitation of conventional cinematic reason, through participation and observation. Not only does the director become part of the film; we can also get an impression of how his presence alters the situations exposed. Nichols emphasizes with very good intuition what happens in such a situation: "The author comes out from behind the external voice commentary, moves away from the poetic vision, slips from the hiding places of the cameras and becomes a social actor, part of the film, like any other "(Introduction to Documentary, 58).

While the author of poetic documentaries delves into intimate, conceptualized, fictionalized subjects, the one of participatory documentary prefers social topics, tangible, easy to approach and capture with the help of the camera. Reality becomes a mundane element that we all know.

The anthropological study is often found in participatory documentaries because the filmmaker can interact with others both through his direct presence among people and by observing and studying. The viewer follows how the films and subjects interact with each other ("Participatory and Reflexive Modes of Documentary: Response 4").

"Filmmakers who seek to represent their direct encounter with the world around them, those who try to represent social aspects and historical perspectives through interviews and the making of compilation films are two major levels of participatory mode. As spectators, we have the impression that we are witnessing a form of a dialogue between the film's director and the subject that emphasizes the commitment made, the negotiated interaction, and the emotion resulting from this meeting. These qualities give the participatory way of making documentaries considerable energy, given the fact that it has a great variety of characters. "
(Introduction to Documentary, 34)

Among the most popular films of this mode, we mention Man with a Camera (1929), The Chronicle of a Summer (1960), and Sherman's March (1985), made throughout the historical period of documentary film (Introduction to Documentary, 34).

The film Chronicle of a Summer is a documentary made in the summer of 1960, by sociologist and anthropologist Edgar Morin and filmmaker Jean Rouch, under the technical and aesthetic baton of director-cameraman Michel Brault. The film begins with a discussion between Rouch and Morin, in which the possibility of a sincere presence in front of the camera is debated. Then, a cast of actual people is introduced to the scene, being questioned by the filmmakers, to discover various intimacies of French society and the level of happiness of the working class. The film is also widely considered being one of the experimental films with an innovative structure and an authentic example of ciné-vérité.

This documentary is the complete opposite of observational documentaries, being very intrusive. Being often filmed by hand, with light and simple cameras, the images can be shaky or of lower quality. Such documentaries require the interviewee to be very open and to answer all the questions the interviewer asks. Unlike observational documentary and poetic documentary, in participatory documentary reality is no longer directed step by step, it is not exploited to extract emotions, reality becomes a spontaneous impression, derived directly from the social fact. The way the characters interact, tell their stories, or exist in front of the camera becomes our reality. Let's not get it wrong, there is also a certain direction in these films in the choice of questions or filming places, but they do not take precedence over the anthropological, social reality recorded. The participatory documentary does not sell us a reality. It shows us, in great detail, that the entire interaction between the film crew and the various interviewees is part of the reality of documentary film production.

The reporter speaks directly with the viewer or the interviewee. The director interacts with the subjects. For example, in North Nanook, Flaherty did not interact on-screen with the filmed characters. In the documentary Photographic Memory (Ross McElwee, 2011), however, the director interacts with his son all the time. The interaction in these films changes from reporter to subject and from material to spectator.

The participatory mode is often described as the one that holds the truest because it admits observation and intervention in the filmed reality. This allows the viewer to experience the existence of a scenario in a given situation and how it changes (Introduction to Documentary, 118). The anthropological study is common in participatory documentaries because the filmmaker can interact both by living among people and by observing and studying a certain socio-anthropological problem, as we have already noted above.

However, we should not be completely impressed by the features of this documentary. The representation of the reality in which we admit the production team has an effect of distancing the spectator from the subject. Although the spontaneous way in which the characters and the film crew interact anchors us in action, the public's constant awareness throughout the film that the entire material is a simple video distorts the relationship between the viewer and the film situation.

3.4. Where the aesthetics of the poetic documentary meets the reflexive

The reflective does not appear as a transparent window on the world, but rather, drawing attention to its constructions and the fact that art and, implicitly, film exist only as a representation of reality. "How is the world painted by documentaries?" is the key question for this kind of movie. It is also the deepest form of documentary - as a self-awareness - and makes us extremely skeptical about the state of objective reality present in the film.

The reflective documentary can take both a formal and political perspective. From a formal perspective, reflexivity draws our attention to our hypotheses and expectations about the form of the film itself (Bucha). From a political perspective, reflexivity indicates our assumptions and expectations about the historical world more than about the form of the film (Bucha).

The reflective documentary is more about the relationship between the director and the audience, showing that the man behind the curtain should change the core of the whole process of the story, as in the glamorous stories of Sarah Polley (Anderson-Moore). Specifically, the way we perceive reality or the events presented in the film is the central goal of this mode.

We return to the poetic documentary and see that this emphasis on form, which the reflexive mode has in the construction of the documentary film, is similar to that present in the construction of the poetic mode. How situations, information, etc. are presented to us. it is certainly more important in reflective and poetic documentaries than in observational, expository, or participatory documentaries.

One of the best-known films made in this way is Land Without Bread (1933). Before shedding light on the fundamental issues that interest us, I would like to argue why this film, in my opinion (as well as Nichols's), respects the structure of the reflexive mode: the self-ironic capacity of the external voice makes us reflect on the subject presented consciously and to understand why the film (in general) is just a representation of reality.

Buñuel, who decided to make the film after reading the ethnographic study Las Jurdes: Étude de Géographie Humaine (1927) by Maurice Legendre, devised a surreal approach to the notion of the anthropological expedition. The result was a documentary film in the form of a travel diary in which the narrator projects himself into the skin of an exaggerated voice that describes in the same tone the miserable conditions in Las Hurdes, the whole monologue being contrasted by the flat and disinterested manner of editing (Ruoff 47).

Conceptualizing and choosing an original way to convey a representation is again a feature that we encounter mainly in the poetic way, where the author's ability to rethink reality and re-establish it according to certain criteria is one of the important pillars that stand at the basis of the production of this documentary mode.

Regarding the pre-production of the film, Buñuel stated:

"I was able to film Las Hurdes thanks to Ramon Acin, an anarchist from Huesca, [...] who, one day, at a café in Zaragoza, said to me: 'Luis, if I ever win a lottery, I would put my money to work to make a movie".

He earned a hundred thousand pesetas and gave me twenty thousand to make this film. With four thousand, I bought a Fiat and made the rest of the film."

(Buñuel)

Although some film researchers describe it as part of the exhibition mode, Land Without Bread is, in fact, according to the studies of Jeffrey Ruoff, an early parody of the newly invented genre (Ruoff 47). We see even from Buñuel's words the self-ironic way he treats the production of this film.

The emotions and empathy we should have felt about the state of generalized poverty are nullified, abolished, from the very beginning of the film, by the tone parodic used and assumed. This is also the fundamental capacity of the reflexive, to destroy a stereotype of cinematic construction, which the poet hardly tries to build.

Nichols notes in his book some important aspects that should also be mentioned:

"The reflexive mode is the most conscious and self-interrogating. Realistic access to the world, the ability to provide convincing evidence, the link between a clue and what it represents - all these notions fall under the label of suspicion. Such notions may force the reflective documentary to examine the nature of this belief, rather than to attest to the validity of what is believed. How the reflective documentary excels refers to directing the viewer towards a superior form of consciousness in terms of his relationship with a documentary and what it represents. " (Introduction to Documentary, 126)

Unlike previous ways of documenting, this way not only pays attention to what is represented but also to the way things are presented.

A very good example of this type of trend is found in Surname Viet Given Name Nam (1989) by Trinh T. Minh-ha. The film is based on interviews with women in Vietnam to describe the oppressive conditions they were forced to face since the end of the war; however, later in the film, the audience learns that these "interviews" of experiences are directing of scenes played by American Vietnamese immigrants. The interviews were initially conducted in Vietnam by someone else with other women and then transcribed and edited by Minh-ha. This shows a conscious effort to have control over what is received by the audience and how the message is imprinted in the consciences of the viewers. In other words, what else but factual information helps in our understanding of the world around us? Instead of questioning knowledge itself, the reflective way of documenting calls into question the principles underlying traditional films and social representations.

The attention that falls on the concept to the detriment of the content indicates the relationship between poetic and reflexive. Higher awareness of reality and its representation is the main feature of the mentioned documentary film modes. How the poet manages to carry his audience through a labyrinth of emotions carefully connected and conceptually directed to offer the audience a solution of self-knowledge and to challenge reality is the same as the ironic and self-analytical aspects of the reflexive mode.

3.5. The performative or the mode closest to the poetic

The documentary in this category is a controversial approach to reality by the filmmaker, born of stress, subjective experience, and emotional response to social life. Strongly personalized and unconventional, slightly experimental, the performance documentary includes events meant to make us taste life from radical perspectives different from what we are used to.

The important difference seems to be that if in the participatory mode the director takes part in the story's construction, but tries to build truths that should be obvious to everyone, the performative mode engages the director, but builds subjective truths significant to him as a person. (Introduction to Documentary, 34).

Very personal and original, the performative mode is suitable for telling the stories of film producers from marginalized social groups, giving them the chance to propagate unique perspectives without having to support the validity of their experiences through aim or aim evidence (Introduction to Documentary, 34).

This subgenre itself could also be attributed to groups (eg women, ethnic minorities, gays and lesbians, etc.), to give them freedom of unconventional expression. Often, an entire arsenal of techniques, many borrowed from fiction or avant-garde films, are used in performance documentaries to link personal experiences to far-reaching political or historical realities.

In the performative mode, the director offers a strong perspective, helping us to discover a culture or an event in history that the public would never know in other ways. In Tongues Untied (1989), African-American director Marlon Riggs combines topicality and personal vision to shed new light on homosexuality in America (Biesterfeld). Also in the performative category are the works of some producers who put together "found footage", such as Péter Forgács from Hungary (Danube Exodus, 1999). His films are created from video files filmed by amateurs as personal recordings, Forgács' films linking these materials to tell the story of ordinary people whose lives are about to be overtaken by catastrophic historical events (Biesterfeld).

The performative mode is also manifested in ethnographic films, such as The Incidents of Travel in Chichen Itza by Jeff Himpele and Quetzal Castañeda. In this visual ethnography of the cultural event of the spring equinox which involves a new form of tourism in a sacred Mayan site in Mexico, ethnographers document the event and offer an ethnographic interrogation of projected meanings on physical heritage objects that attract 50,000 tourists. period of the Chichen equinox (Simple and Castañeda). Here, unlike Michael Moore's performative documentaries, in which there are a specific message and argument, an open polyphonic film is created, in which the audience is more likely to define the meanings, messages, and understanding of what they represent the movie.

Documentaries, in particular educational documentaries, are written in such a way that the public is persuaded to accept a specific lesson or message. The performative mode of documentation is used to detach from a single or monotonous understanding, not only by using the dialogical principles of dialogic anthropology but also by experimental ethnography (Himpele and Castañeda). Thus, Himpele and Castañeda create an ethnographic documentary that expands experimental ethnography as a set of principles regarding the writing of a text for the production and post-production of ethnographic film.

The documentary is constantly driven by film conventions and ideologies. Even the best intentions can bring a manipulation of the experiences recorded by the screenwriter; if the message of a documentary is unclear, it will have little impact; however, the nature of the exhibition is defined in the ease of interpretation of its message ("Performative Documentary Characteristics"). The most authoritarian of the modes, the expository one, presents its story with an argumentative approach, credible, but still subject to artistic deviations ("Performative Documentary Characteristics"). The performative mode tries to avoid this trap by presenting the narrative as a personal journey, a struggle, or a search that begins and ends throughout the film ("Performative Documentary Characteristics").

Filmmakers strive to represent reality as authentically as possible, trying to find a balance between unedited images and the need to generate a finished, informative, marketable product.

To better understand the stakes and significance of performative documentary, a few words from John Arthur Little's The Power and Potential of Performative Documentary Film, in the section in which he tries to find appropriate definitions, should be transcribed here:

"Traditional narrative structures usually present a problem and then offer a solution. It shows us a historical world (character, event, condition, etc.) that serves as a reference in the relationship between director, film, and spectator.

The traditional documentary refers more to the message sent to the viewer, the message induced by the film to the viewer to be perceived. Transmission to and induction are important words because the difference between deduction/induction and transmission/reception is at the heart of what differentiates performative documentary from traditional documentary ...

The difference between the viewer of a traditional documentary and a performative documentary is well served by this analogy: it is the difference between being a member of a jury listening to the complete argument prepared by a lawyer explaining the significance of the evidence and being the lawyer himself to investigate. and examine each clue to collect or extract meaning from the body of evidence. "

(Little 28)

Now, after we managed to point out some important aspects related to the performative documentary, we have to see how it influences, interacts with the poetic documentary. We also brought to light during the previous chapters the fact that certain passages, treated in the format of the poetic documentary, are integrated with other genres of documentaries. Even in Michael Moore's performance documentary, Fahrenheit 9/11, we have such moments as we mentioned earlier.

We see, thus, that the performative documentary tries to reinvent itself and to find, on the go, creative solutions. Film styles and genres become obsolete and uninteresting as viewers become bored with a format they are used to.

There is a global trend in approaching new ways of representing and structuring documentaries, to make them more attractive to the public. Thus, the poetic documentary manages to become a source of inspiration for creators. Focused especially on the form in which emotion, information, or state is transmitted, he manages to open the doors to a world of self-knowledge and experimentation. This self-knowledge and experimentation are the starting point of the new forms of documentary that have appeared in recent years and which we will talk about in detail in the following chapters.

3.6. Experimental film, visual essay, or poetic documentary

I would like to review some important elements that differentiate the poetic documentary from the video essay or experimental film. This operation of terminological circumscription is necessary for even better fixation of the content of the concepts with which I decided to operate throughout this paper.

If we talk about the visual essay, Ligia Smarandache reminds us in the summary of the doctoral thesis entitled The Role of the Video Essay in Postmodern Audiovisual Communication (2011) the following characteristics:

„- is a form of knowledge between theory (science) and art;
- has an introspective, self-reflective character;
- does not follow a formal method;
- it is a process of organizing complexity;
- captures transient processes;
- communicates abstract ideas, intangible thoughts, and notions;
- has a nonlinear structure;
- is interested in the processes behind the actions. "

(Smarandache 6)

We see that, in the enumerated characteristics, the representation of the real is not an obligatory condition (practically, it does not even exist as a characteristic), while in the poetic documentary it is the fundamental act of constituting the discourse. On the other hand, many of the characteristics of the visual essay are also common to the poetic documentary, as we can deduce from the list above, which is not - of course - exhaustive in any form.

To better understand the relationship between the visual essay and the poetic documentary, I propose for analysis of the visual essay made by Ligia Smarandache entitled Confessions (Confessions, 2011). We see, since the opening of this film, that the whole concept focuses on several main landmarks: the screen is divided in two, on the left is projected an animated film by removing the background, and on the right, we see symbolic or random images which visually support the external voice. The external voice, which is often required for a visual essay, presents "a series of existential questions about the meaning of our life and our passage through it" (Confessions). The symbol images on the right are each associated with a complex cultural significance: the group of crows that sits on the roof of the block is associated with death, both culturally and through the external voice; images of a horse rider suggest the journey through life, and the image of a child preparing to draw symbolizes the creative spirit of a man trying to build concepts and images through the process of filtering information through the senses (according to the external voice in the film).

On the left side of the screen, the silhouette of the abstracted character performs various positions or movements in relation to the message transmitted by the external voice, moving from one space to another, duplicating or teleporting through various technical procedures. The two projections, the real one on the right and the abstract one on the left, visually support the external voice. Even if the images on the right represent real situations, they are not structured in such a way as to construct a certain reality, being mixed according to the visual support requirements issued by the external voice and not being documentary (nor were they selected and juxtaposed for this purpose).

Similar to the experimental film in this respect, the visual essay is not obliged to be based on a real story like the documentary films, which makes the visual essay able to adopt a very abstract concept throughout it. Breaking reality is not necessarily mandatory. Given that many of the visual essays include an external voice, it can present an abstract, philosophical text superimposed over as real, tangible images as possible. As for the experimental film, it is by the very name of a pure experiment, so it can not be included in the category of a well-defined project with a structure based on reality.

"Experimental film is difficult to define, not because its orientations are so abstract or even esoteric, but because it is such a vast genre that its definition almost exceeds the purpose of the genre itself. In a sense, it refers to any element that defies the conventions of traditional narrative and documentary cinema. He doesn't have to tell a story. It doesn't have to have characters. It doesn't even have to be a message of any kind. It can be visceral or every day, engaging or completely boring. It can be extremely personal or political. It can be anything."

(Hardy, 2013)

We understand that the experimental film does not have clear rules; it does not have to follow any rules. If the visual essay has certain characteristics or uses certain elements of cinematic language, with the experimental film there is no limit imposed by the genre.

One of the important films of universal cinema, Meshes of the Afternoon (1943), directed by Maya Deren and Alexander Hammid, shows us how experimental film, present in history since the beginnings of cinema, imposes itself as an independent genre in an industry that does not it leaves a lot of room for expression for filmmakers who would like to practice it, through the monopolies held by the big production houses. In this film, we are described as a dream of a woman in which several symbolic elements are presented successively and circularly. The authors opted for a conventional narrative, with characters, action, and music, then restructured it into a circular story, repeating certain images, using a non-drum editing rhythm, and using unusual camera angles to make everyday objects take on a symbolic character. These stylistic features are now easy to highlight in the works of directors such as David Lynch or Barbara Hammer. The symbol images used in that film were then taken over by pop culture through music videos (for example, Ambling Alp).

We notice that although it is not a genre known and appreciated by the public, the experimental is the promoter of new ideas, which are then partially or taken over by cinema and the media. Using symbols and visual concepts are the basic elements in the construction of these films, even if many of the experimental films do not use such actual images or use ordinary objects in the construction of sequences. Because of these aspects, there is a tendency to associate or confuse poetic documentaries with experimental ones. The confusion occurs when the viewer does not appeal to the representation of reality, so if we take as an example Meshes of the Afternoon we can easily see that the film does not present a real, tangible situation,

The main difference between poetic mode and experimental films is that the poetic mode does not deny the classical style of editing, image exposure, filming, cropping on frames or camera movements and does not seek to discover other forms or elements of cinematic language, but it focuses its attention on the subjective way in which life is perceived. The poetic documentary respects these conventions, most of the time, and even if it emphasizes more on form than on content, this way of documentary approaches a real theme, whether it is about spirituality, life, death, animals, people dance. or anything else. The experimental film, by its definition, is a manifesto against the classic style of making a film, through editing, image, directorial concept, script, theme, or scenography.

I will not dwell too much on the definitions and classifications of experimental films or visual essays, because that is not the purpose of this thesis. What I wanted to emphasize through this brief comparison is that the documentary, no matter how it is approached (expository, reflective, poetic, etc.), always directs attention to reality or to the ideas we have about it in different cultural eras. . The documentary has its origin in the palpable, tangible reality, no matter how manipulated its content is or how truncated the facts from which it is inspired are truncated.

4. Poetic documentary: another way of visual expression

The poetic mode does not refer to the "objective" reality of a given situation or of people, but it proposes - instead - to understand an inner "truth" that can only be achieved through poetic manipulation. It depends exclusively on the documentary producers to build their narrative (or non-narrative) structure appropriate to the target audience.

Laurențiu Damian talks to us in his work (published in 2003) about the poetic documentary, calling it "documentary-essay". The author informs us that he comes to complete, through image, word, sound elements (noise, music) the representation of that "beyond reality" (Damian 188).

Even if many of the poetic documentaries do not follow a classical narrative structure, their construction has a natural tendency to form certain patterns to convey a message. Therefore, in this chapter, the emphasis will be on the patterns implemented by the authors, in the realization of the mentioned genre of films. The present approach involves an analysis, under the lens of insight, of several aspects, such as rhythmicity, relation to cinematic time, the use of colors and lights, connecting elements, as well as dialogue or any verbal source used in the narrative structure.

The analysis of the image practiced since ancient times in the case of painting becomes in the XX and XXI centuries a means to discern the intentions of the creator, but also a way to operate with its own set of cultural-aesthetic values, which we use daily in our interaction with images. Ever since the cave paintings, the image has remained how humanity transmitted information, emotions, and aesthetic values, how visual culture was shaped, increased, and declined, with the emergence of new aesthetic paradigms or techniques for generating, recording, or processing the image. The operation of dissecting the narrative structure on which the poetic documentary is based and which I will try in the following pages aims at systematization and classification of the dramatic elements that define the genre (Ruby 47).

We will return to our research on the introductory considerations we have undertaken in the previous chapter on the poetic mode, trying to draw a broader and more precise trajectory of this mode, from its appearance to the present day. So, I started by referring to the specific features, analyzing some examples from the history of the documentary film like Regen, Symphony City, or Samsara.

Following the course of this way of making documentaries, we can see how their aesthetics change depending on certain historical-cultural and technical features. The best example to analyze is the case of Stan Brakhage, whose interest in poetic documentary and documentary film was extremely intense and systematic.

Brakhage made his film debut with the film Interim (1953), a fictional drama, without dialogue, atypically built for that time. Dialogue films have existed, as we know, since 1927 ("The History of Sound at the Movies"). Although the dialogue appears in certain sequences in a visual format (the actors talk to each other), the director chooses not to introduce the related sound in the film. The emphasis on the visual construction of the film, on the relationships between the elements that appear on the screen, is the cornerstone on which Stan Brakhage will build his entire career.

One of his first poetic documentaries was Window Water Baby Moving (1959), a film that marked the history of cinema. I consider it necessary to mention the context in which this film was made, because, as we specified in the previous chapter, the poetic documentary is a very subjective interpretation of reality, assumed by the creator.

Stan Brakhage's wife, Jane, had insisted that Brakhage be present at the birth of their daughter (MacDonald, "A Critical Cinema. 5 Interviews with Independent Filmmakers"). The hospital where she was to give birth initially granted permission to film, but it was later withdrawn. Instead, Brakhage transferred the birth home, paying for a nurse and some expensive emergency equipment (MacDonald, "A Critical Cinema. 5 Interviews with Independent Filmmakers"). Jane was initially shy about filming but eventually changed her mind after Brakhage made a dramatic scene.

Most of the film was shot by Brakhage himself, Jane occasionally took the camera to capture her husband's reactions (MacDonald, "A Critical Cinema. 5 Interviews with Independent Filmmakers"). The editing of the film lasted several months and was done in the evening. According to Brakhage, a new delay was caused when Kodak processed the film. Brakhage described the event as follows:

"When I sent them the footage for processing, Kodak responded with a letter that said more or less," Sign this document at the bottom and we'll destroy this film; otherwise, we will hand him over to the police." So the doctor replied with a letter that the film was made for medical purposes and I recovered the bruises. "

Brakhage later felt that Window Water Baby Moving insufficiently captured the emotions at the birth of his child and, during the birth of his third child, filmed Thigh Line Lyre Triangular (1961) as an improvement (MacDonald, "A Critical Cinema. 5 Interviews with Independent Filmmakers ").

We notice that Window Water Baby Moving is not just a personal experience, a fragment of life was put into images but is a set of subjective experiences that substantially change the final version of the film. Unlike fiction films, where most of the time the scenery is carefully thought out in a certain way, and the sequence of frames and the involvement of the characters in the story must serve specific purposes, in Brakhage, the whole film must be adapted to the situation.

The first deviation from the initial concept is the hospital's denial of the right to film on the premises. The first subjective aspect is that the author does not film any birth, but the birth of his child. Another important aspect is the filming by himself and by the main character (his wife, by the way) who lives, lives, a birth.

The invention of the reason for recovering Kodak's brutes, as well as the editing in the evening, also by him (who appears in this film as a screenwriter, director, cameraman, actor, etc.), after finishing his official activity on the current day, become part of the movie.

His film is, in essence, a documentary that follows the birth of a child, but the way it is filmed, directed, edited, etc. turns the film into an attempt to capture the emotions and feelings related to this common and yet each time unique event.

Just as we discussed in the first chapter about raising a man from the everyday banality to romantic art, the author's film turns our attention to this important aspect, showing us how our struggle with problems and daily life makes us heroes of our destinies. This struggle becomes not only the main subject of the cinematographic work but also a way of exploring the inner world, of understanding its complex meanders.

One of Stan Brakhage's later films, The Act of Seeing with One's Own Eyes (1971), documents the extremely visually appealing autopsy procedures used by forensic doctors, such as organ removal and the embalming process. This film has been described as an observation and immersion study (Hall), a critic considering Brakhage a documentary of subjectivity, who uses film techniques to "shape his eye" (Camper). This critic argues that the main purpose of the film is to "sensitize each viewer to his subjectivity" (Camper).

After all, this is one of the characteristics of the poetic documentary. The spectator's awareness of his subjectivity is the starting point from which this way of the documentary is built. Starting from the mentioned premise, the form and the concept itself try to capitalize on the aesthetic capacity of the images presented, at a maximum level, through the specific elements of cinematic language. Most of

Brakhage's films are constructed purely visually, without the use of any sound.

While the film about autopsies is, by its nature, shocking and sometimes difficult to watch, it is far from a film that exploits certain sensationalism. It invites us to meditate on life, death, the body, on how fragile we all are, while people's organs are removed, leaving only empty cranial cavities or dried bodies on the inside. What is a human being? Who were these people in everyday life? Why is it so difficult to watch a movie that talks about us, about our (in) organic existence? Brakhage raises all these questions and lets us meditate on the human being.

The last film in the author's filmography that we will subject to a brief analysis is Scenes from Under Childhood (1967).

Brakhage's marriage to Jane Collom, the subsequent birth of their five children, and moving to Colorado, rural areas, inspired the director to document family life in an extremely personal and challenging way. In the highly articulated and dramatized scenes from the film, Brakhage tries to visualize the child's psychological interior as he discovers the world around him, from birth to adulthood.

The symbols, which we will talk about in the rest of the work, play an important role in his films. Fields of organic colors that represent the mother's womb, visually distorted impressions of the physical world, in the author's vision, materializing the social space and aspects of the descriptive order that Brakhage tried to bring to light so eloquently throughout his career. Visual symbols are not limited to the boundaries imposed by the culture in which Brakhage produces these films, managing to develop a series of symbols and associations, different and much more complex, through his visual experiments. As we know, both Brakhage and Maya Deren (about whom we will talk immediately) made both poetic documentaries and experimental films.

Scenes from Under Childhood is, in fact, a series of films made on 16 mm support in four independent sections by the producer Stan Brakhage, between 1967 and 1970. All four sections are without soundtrack, although Brakhage has developed a sound version, available for the first section. In a 2008 magazine called Village Voice, critic J. Hoberman described the film as "a glorious, romantic, two-hour and something epic" (Hoberman).

When asked to describe the film, Brakhage himself wrote that it was:

"A view of the inner world of the beginnings of the fetus, the baby, the child, in short - a rupture of the "myths of childhood" by revealing the extremes of violent terror and the overwhelming joy of this world materialized in the minds of adults through their feelings-related memory. " ("Catalog / Scenes From Under Childhood: Section No. 1")

We observe, thus, that the author's intention is clear in making a poetic documentary, even if at that time there was no obvious theoretical distinction regarding the classifications of documentary film in ways. His option in making a poetic documentary at the expense of a visual essay or experimental film is found in maintaining a consistent representation of reality throughout that series of films.

If we refer to the poetic mode of the documentary film, we must bring into discussion Maya Deren, a complete artist, about whom much has been written and who has remained in the world of cinema as a landmark for contemporary filmmakers. Deren is best known for his experimental films, as mentioned above, which is very important due to the intimate relationship between experimental film and poetic documentary.

In the spring of 1945, she conducted A Study in Choreography for Camera which Deren said was "an effort to isolate and celebrate the principle of the power of motion" (Kay and Peary). The different compositions and speeds of the frame movement interact with Deren's meticulous changes and the different speeds of the film to create a dance that in

149

the artist's view could only exist in the film. Encouraged the dynamics of movement are greater than anything else in the film, Maya Deren established a completely new meaning of the word "geography" because the dancer's movement transcends and manipulates the ideas of time (Kay and Peary). Since the film lasts only 3 minutes, this project is probably a fragment (from a broader perspective),

The choreography is perfectly synchronized as it appears seamlessly in an outdoor courtyard and then returns to an open natural space. It shows an evolution from nature to the limits of society and back to nature. The character belongs to dancer and choreographer Talley Beatty, whose latest move is a leap across the screen back into the natural world. The editing of the film is broken, it presents different angles and compositions and even parts filmed in slow motion, and through these aspects, Deren can keep the quality of the jump smooth and seemingly uninterrupted.

The attempt to render the continuity of the dancer's movement as a real, palpable element, from one scene to another, makes this short film fall even in the form of a study in the category of poetic documentary through aesthetics and the approached theme.

Another important achievement is The Private Life of a Cat, a 1944 silent film directed by Maya

Deren and Alexander Hammid. Using their cats in their apartment, they try to detail the intimate world of these cats. A few brief text inserts easily structure the trials and challenges facing the new kitten. Cutting the images into detailed shots and channeling the attention to the movement creates an intimate communication between the spectator and the "protagonists". The intimate, subjective approach lived through the prism of the complete cut-out, influenced by the relationship between the master-director and the characters-protagonists, respects the same "recipe" that I observed in Brakhage's case. The director has absolute control of all stages of making the film. The action takes place in a controlled, intimate, subjective space.

    I would like to review how the subject of this film is approached from a poetic perspective. An excellent scene is when we see the mother giving birth and how she cleans the five newborn kittens with her tongue. We see that in the banality of a daily event, Hammid also deals with some important themes of the existence of our society, such as birth. Even if this event is no longer the author's personal experience (as in Brakhage's film) our intrusion into the intimate world of animal characters makes sensory stimulation an equally personal experience. The documentary becomes a subjective projection in which scientific data or aim, measurable perspectives are lost in contrast to the effective approach, channeled on emotion and form.

Next, we will talk about Godfrey Reggio, another important director of the poetic mode. Reggio is best known for the Qatsi (Life) trilogy, which includes the films Koyaanisqatsi, Powaqqatsi, and Naqoyqatsi. All film titles are taken from the Hopi language, Koyaanisqatsi meaning "life out of balance", Powaqqatsi meaning "life in transformation", and Naqoyqatsi meaning "life as war". Reggio spent fourteen years in fasting, silence, and prayer, training to be a monk in the Congregation of Christian Brothers, a Roman Catholic pontifical order, before abandoning this path and making films. If we follow his trilogy, which we will analyze in the following paragraphs, we will be able to observe how his 14 years of experience spent in contemplation make its mark on the topics addressed, but also on how these films are made. The vision of the world that Reggio transposes through images is a vision as subjective as it is broad.

Unlike the poetic documentaries discussed above, at Godfrey Reggio music becomes an important pillar in structure. Ambient, experimental sounds, instrumental music, as well as various other sounds, are harmoniously integrated to support the image. We see that the world described by these documentaries is no longer a city street, a family of cats, a morgue, or the birth of a child. The universe of Godfrey's documentaries is infinite. From distant stars to the microscopic world, everything makes up a whole that tells a story.

Reggio said that Qatsi films intend to simply create an experience and that the viewer must develop a theory of the meaning of the film (Carson) on his own. He also added that these films did not have as their central theme the effect of technology, of industry on people, but the fact that everything exists within technology, it becoming ubiquitous like the air we breathe (Carson).

Koyaanisqatsi consists, first of all, of slow-motion recordings of the cities and natural landscapes of the United States. The visual poem contains neither dialogue nor vocal narration: its tone is set by the juxtaposition of images and music. Reggio explained the lack of dialogue, stating that "the lack of emotion of the language is not the reason why these films have no words, but because ... our language is in a general state of humiliation. It no longer describes the world we live in. " (Carson).

The film is a careful examination of modern life, in all its ugliness and poetic beauty. Reggio's vision is full of double images, both worldly and profound: the sky and the oceans, the cities and the microchips, the factory conveyor belts, and the subway escalators (Wilkie). The film juxtaposes the natural world with the intertwining artificial world;

living, pulsating, cities frighten us with scenes of poverty and urban decay (Wilkie). Reggio presents the twin subjects, human triumph, and human failure, suggesting that we tip the scales towards the latter as we travel on the path to ecological catastrophe (Wilkie).

While Koyaanisqatsi has focused on modern life in industrialized countries, Powaqqatsi, which similarly has no dialogue, focuses more on the conflict in third world countries between traditional ways of life and the new ways of life introduced. with industrialization. As with Koyaanisqatsi and the third and final part of the trilogy, Naqoyqatsi, the film is closely linked to the soundtrack, written by Philip Glass. Here, human voices (especially children, especially from South America and Africa) appear more than in Koyaanisqatsi, in harmony with the message and images of the film.

This time the theme appears in a more deliberate way and with less ambiguity, or even abstraction, than in the previous film. The opposition of several cultural elements, such as religion or political organization, is more obvious.

The film begins with images of various manual trades in developing countries in South America and Africa. These are most often filmed in slow motion as if the fast-forward motion that dominated the first film has not yet been discovered (Cettl). From the aforementioned images appear illustrations of a collective cultural identity or religious rituals and practices performed in the middle of homes (Cettl). Slowly, the wild and beautiful land is divided and irrigated, as the "progress" of Western development is fulfilled, transforming the lives of those it affects them (Smith). Cultural harmony with nature is eroded, and the image of a fast-forward image of a train becomes the bridge to another journey, as Western life, again, tries to dominate the landscape and the people (Cettl).

Images of Western culture are now penetrating and the population is being pushed into dissonance, constantly looking at the camera as if deliberately interrogated. Urban development and the progress made by these people go beyond their simplicity, forcing their perspective on life.

Naqoyqatsi, the last film in the series, focuses on the digital age and how humanity is slowly losing its connection with nature. From scenes of abandoned buildings to science labs, everything we see is cold and far removed from natural reality.

Naqoyqatsi focuses on several aspects of his thesis "Life in War". There is an obvious interpretation - the statement that man's violent tendencies and self-destructive character will soon take the perfect form (Vice). The film also seeks to explain the role that technology has played in this path of humanity, as well as to develop the debate over whether genetic experimentation is ethical or a violation of natural law (Vice). Reggio and his team of editing, animation, and filming use such tricks as thermal imaging, X-ray photography, and distorted digital images, which sometimes work well (Vice).

We notice that the documentaries of the poetic mode evolved with the development of cinematographic techniques. In addition to this aspect, they kept their strongly subjectivized character. The director's vision is still the central element in the construction of the film. The choice of themes, subjects, and editing are kept in the same format, focused on raising awareness of the subjectivity of viewers. As for the theme approached, like pointed out above, it tries to include global, general themes (a feature, in fact, specific to most documentaries after the 2000s), a phenomenon distinct from the poetic documentaries before the 80s. existing remain, most of the time, in a timeless stage, unresolved; we only see their existence. The same structure of the subject is preserved, which does not have the role of "teaching us something", but of making us aware of certain things that usually go unnoticed. If the sound of the film was almost completely missing from the first poetic documentaries, it returns in recent films in the form of ambient, experimental, or instrumental sounds.

The editing takes advantage of technological developments and adopts a freestyle, manipulating cinematic time and space by cutting short or long frames, accelerating or slowing down the playback speed.

Another very important aspect is the diversity of the topics approached, but also of the approaches. If in direct cinema or other documentary film concepts the use of lights, filming angles, characters, etc. follows a certain logic, we notice that in the poetic documentary the structure or approach of the subject (with or without external voice, with or without sound, rhythmic editing on music or not, filming with the camera in hand or on a tripod, etc.) differs very a lot. Directors approach a wide range of artistic techniques and processes, using all the resources that cinematic language has at their disposal, even inventing new resources, if necessary, in this creative process.

The poetic mode allows itself, by its experimental nature, to approach or create another way of representing reality, with the risk of being or not to the affinity of the public. Thus, we see how this way of documentary preserves its integrity and continuity not only beyond the era of the film but also in the era of virtual reality or the concept of cloud filmmaking. The poetic approach is a necessary pillar in the development of cinematography through its innovative capacity, regardless of the environment in which the representation is made.

4.1. Symbolism in poetic documentary

The exploration of spatiality and forms, beyond the barriers imposed by cultural dogmas, generates a new direction of contemplation. Forms become true treasures of visual culture, in which meanings and non-meanings intertwine to destroy the stereotypical thinking of filmmakers.

A powerful symbol, present and promoted in modern poetic documentaries, is encountered in various forms and sequences throughout them. We refer to spirituality, religion, or how mankind philosophically relates to its existence.

The spectacular example presented in this chapter is the series of sequences from the movie Samsara, between 80-90 minutes. Here we get acquainted with the connection with divinity through prayer, specific to the four great global religions: Jewish, Muslim, Christian, and Buddhist.

Although the film begins by presenting this "story" from the perspective of the Buddhist religion (begins and ends with specific rituals), the successive way in which various moments during the prayers of each religion are described shows the similarities that can be found between seemingly very different religious systems. . As religion is a powerful reservoir of symbols exploited in this type of poetic documentary, beyond aesthetic appearances, it has a strong effect on our subjectivity and on the way we decipher the content of films.

The symbol, used in the ancient culture to represent something in a simple and easy to decode by the great mass of the population (as we mentioned in Subchapter 1.1.) Acquires an impressive value especially during the documentaries in the Qatsi trilogy.

Nature is presented as a support for reality; basically, this is where "our story" begins. How nature, as a symbol of eternity in film, is shaped, processed, transformed, destroyed by man represents how we relate to this reality. For example, in Powaqqatsi we have a series of sequences (in the opening of the film) with people carrying, loading, working on the processing and exploitation of nature. This series is presented in a dynamic rhythm, in line with the images of an erupting volcano. The destructive force of nature itself is associated with human nature, just as destructive and unstoppable from its constant actions of transforming the environment.

In addition to religion and nature, another symbol often used is that of the uniform as a way of social organization. From the military uniforms of the military in the conflict zones between Israel and Palestine (Samsara, minute 80), the colorful uniforms from the military parades (minute 77), the uniforms of the detainees (minute 64), the sports uniforms (Naqoyqatsi, minute 22), traditional uniforms (Powaqqatsi, minute 99), workers' uniforms (Koyaanisqatsi, minute 54) to the body paintings of various tribes, the authors of these films manage to show us not only the diversity of this symbol of social organization but also the character of the group they define. The characters often do not interact with each other, being presented in formal situations, whether they are in factories or military actions. People move symmetrically, mechanically, in uniforms of the same color and with the same appearance, perform similar actions. Even the tribes, presented in traditional clothing and body decorations, usually perform various symmetrical rituals or identical actions. Belonging to social groups and the action of modeling, organizing, or destroying nature is therefore organized according to certain rules (aesthetic or content).

As we mentioned in Chapter 1, in the passages about the aesthetics of the fine arts in antiquity, symmetry plays an important role in the construction of images. If 2000 years ago symmetry was used, however, to emphasize balance, perfection, harmony, in the films, we are referring to here symmetry is generally used to emphasize mechanization and loss of identity.

Consumerism, mechanization, and accelerating the pace of nature's exploitation is another theme-symbol explored in these films. Accelerating images in contrast to the slow motion effect shows us how, through the process of automation (means of transport, robots, machines) manual, inert mode, presented in its primary form at the beginning of the film Koyaanisqatsi, remains only a vague memory that including developing countries will soon surpass it. Consumerism is also described by the endless technological processes by which clothing, food, or household items are processed (some examples). The multiple repetitive actions never begin and end, they continue with short breaks indefinitely.

The loss of identity is built in these films by the process of accelerating cinematic time, by processing images and adding special effects, exemplifying aesthetic operations (Samsara, minute 58), but also by symbol sequences such as the one from minute 38 (Samsara), in which a man masks his face with a layer of clay.

Also during the film Samsara we discover how a man does not just turn into a machine, performing mechanical operations according to an established schedule, being copied as an aesthetic aspect in sex dolls or robots. Even the theme of sexuality and the sex industry that similarly exploits women is present in Samsara (minute 60) or Baraka (minute 57).

In addition to these aspects, it would be good to mention what is not presented in these documentaries, to understand the difference between classical and modern poetic documentaries in terms of symbolic aspects.

In the classic poetic documentaries are treated, in particular, the aesthetic valences of the human body, of the surrounding world. The symbols present in Deren's or Brakhage's films are rendered subjectively to edit, cutting into frames, or the directorial concept. Cats are personalized, they gain human social traits. The birth of Brakhage's daughter is not only a new beginning of life, but it is also a way in which we can experience this intimate event intensely.

Exploring the minimalist, intimate space of man or animal through the aesthetic means specific to the poetic way, and knowing these characters with their defects and qualities is a strongly invasive artistic approach. These aspects, however, are not found in modern poetic documentaries, where the directorial concept is built following the subject presented neutrally. Detailed shots are rarely present, there are no shots from subjective angles or made "from hand".

4.2. The directorial vision - an aesthetic of cyclicity

The main aspect of the theme approached by the directors of modern poetic documentaries like Mark Magidson or Ron Fricke is the introduction of the spectators in the cyclicity of the material and immaterial forms presented in a global context. Through careful and applied film analysis, we discover how religion or traditional customs are based on common elements that have developed, in parallel, in several cultures worldwide.

From the beginning of cinema, documentarians have been fascinated by cases of architectural failure, human life, and our actions. The personal stories of those affected, reflected in the background of ruins and urban disintegration, provide fertile ground for making documentaries. But this kind of documentary film realizes uniquely the story of how our society decays or is reborn depending on general socio-economic developments.

The poetic documentary reminds us of the subjectivism manifested in the period of romanticism (Chapter 1), namely the extremely personal way in which the author refers to reality. The world around him becomes a malleable mass that is shaped by the filter of cinematic language, to the liking of the artist.

The director's vision differs from documentary to documentary, but during the poetic documentaries, a common feature can be observed, namely: the ability of creators to look beyond the limits that the technical, social, or dogmas of the guild impose. We have deep political, social, demographic, historical, natural visions, which are outlined during this kind of documentation. As in Subchapter 1.1., The limitations regarding the technological process, the general knowledge about the world, the political organization, or the intimate space make the poetic way a true avant-garde source of visual solutions, still helped by the digital age in which we stepped, with all its innovations.

If in the Middle Ages (briefly described in Subchapter 1.3.) political, social, and economic instability left its mark brutally and directly on the aesthetics of the visual arts, we observe the same recurring phenomenon in contemporary aesthetics. The image of war through scenes with great impact force, such as conflict zones, military weapons, war machines, cities destroyed or abandoned because of conflicts, appears sharply in Baraka (minute 67), Koyaanisqatsi (minute 29), Naqoyqatsi (minute 12), Samsara (minute 81).

The directorial vision is an act limited by the possibilities that a creator has when he chooses a certain stylistic and narrative concept. Above all, this irreversibly determines the natural course of images even when we are in the niche of the poetic documentary which implies greater freedom of expression and interpretation. Thus, although much of the criticism of films belonging to this genre states the authors pay little attention to the narrative means characteristic of current cinema, looking in-depth we see rigor in the space-time management of the film, but also the artistic side, represented by editing, music, scenography, chromatics, etc.

Even if the physical universe is limited by the rules that govern it, the narrative means that can be used in the director's development's vision are unlimited. The authors justify the choice of these narrative means, stating that they try to interpret the motives and paradigms completely, at the discretion of the viewer or critic, the author separating, in managing the narrative space, from his ubiquitous capacity for interpretation.

The issues addressed by the representatives of realism that we discussed in this paper, Subchapter 1.6., Namely the immortalization of certain moments in the actual world for moralizing purposes, become the primary engine that often guides the directorial vision of this mode of documentary film. Even if the author does not address us directly through the external voice or interview, the presentation of actual images, with a strong descriptive character, draws us in a certain direction of the way we should interpret the image.

4.3. Global interconnection

From the beginning, we specify that this context of global interconnection applies only to modern poetic documentaries. As mentioned before, the first documentaries focus on intimate, minimalist issues or themes.

The concept of interconnection is the foundation brick in the semantic construction of films made by Ron Fricke, Mark Magidson, Gregory Colbert (Ashes and Snow), Godfrey Reggio, and others. This concept, as part of the director's vision, condenses as a whole the perishable and everyday character of society, represented by the routine activities of people in various spaces and creating a contrasting effect through sustainable elements such as historic buildings or cultural customs that remain unmoved. in the face of the passage of time. Ashes and Snow is a film by Gregory Colbert that evokes a timeless communion between humanity and nature. The connection we have with nature and the planet we were born with is a cleverly exploited theme in this film that reminds us that before digital globalization, we were otherwise connected and to everything around us.

In another context, one of the relevant aspects of the phenomenon of globalization, conceptually structured during the poetic documentaries of other authors, is the random presentation of different societies and their stage of development.

This aspect is relevant because the transition from archaic to modern in the real world is sudden and dissonant.

Societies have a general tendency to free themselves from the pressure of the present continuous and interact to influence each other regardless of their degree of development, a conclusion that emerges from researching the films we have chosen to refer to constantly here. In a review by Josh Spiegel of Samsara, the author argues for the same idea: "A film made of stunning images is also a dissertation on what it means to be alive in a world where we are barely aware of what what is beyond our door. " (Spiegel). In other words, our attempt to become aware of what is happening around us is embedded in our lack of experience and knowledge in the face of the size/immensity of the cosmos.

Beyond the expectations that the film promotion campaign tried to spread, the media remained inert and quite neutral in terms of criticism. The big fight revolved around the fruitful content in the film. Real controversies presented by the Los Angeles Times, the debates aim at the lack of a detailed exposure of the filming places. The article published by Turan argues that this lack is a crucial issue of the film, emphasizing more the informational importance of the documentary (in the content of the article) than its aesthetic character, which is underlined by the author of the film from the first framework.

The ability of films to transcend the barriers of verbal language generates this highly morally punctuated global consciousness by Rogert Eber in his article on the Baraka documentary written for his website: "If humanity sends another Voyager to distant stars and can only carry a film on board, this film should be Baraka "(Eber).

The universal and interconnected character of the chaining of visual elements is essentialized by the very desire of the director and the producer to explore culture as a global phenomenon. This propensity for universality and the unification of cultures is part of the continuous development of the social paradigm, but also the erasure of the boundaries between Christianity and other religions; the unification of religions pursues the goal of unifying the discrepancies that cultures experience. Almost subliminally we discover during the film Samsara the Christian baptism ritual of a newborn from Denmark, but also Buddhist monks, Tibetans, drawing with colored sand mandalas (ritual whose purpose is to celebrate the Earth and humanity), a real frenzy of the show life invites us all to participate "(Fricke and Magidson).

This phenomenon is detailed by the film's producer, Mark Magidson, who opens the horizon of knowledge through his speech in the interview:

"We realized that images simply guide us like a transcendent current, through all the similarities, being under the same content, but in a different form "(" DP / 30: Samsara, filmmakers Ron Fricke & Mark Magidson ", 00: 10: 15-00: 30: 10).

Another feature of the concept of global consciousness is carefully emphasized in the film Samsara by the idea of the movement of groups of people. In the 15th minute of the film we see a group joining in the synchronous dance, bowing or standing, on their knees, with their arms in the air, their fingers fluttering like birds' wings, their voices like a rhythmic chatter, so that towards the end of the film we see an enormous group of followers of the Muslim religion revolving in a circle around the Mecca monument.

Therefore, continuity is ensured by the content; a content whose purpose is to strive for universality. Just as the concept of the pyramid or the connection of the pyramid with a form of divinity appeared on both the African and American continents, without any cultural exchange between these two continents at that time, so the content tends to be rationalized and assimilated by society in a subconscious way.

The return to nature, to the balance between us and the universe, is achieved following the same functional patterns manifested both in realism (the plastic current of the nineteenth century) and in realism manifested in ancient Greece, where the natural model is the only element needed to develop the concept. in the process of creation.

Asked by Earth 2.0 what the Earth would look like in a vision, Mark Magidson responded with an easy-to-anticipate statement: "If people realized we were all on a huge ball of the earth traveling through vast space and empty of the universe and that our supreme need is to work together towards the realization of great ideas, would be all we dreamed "(Silva). One can observe the same vision punctuated so accurately throughout his campaign to promote the process of spiritual unification. The search for a universal language turns into a frantic creative concept, a real game of montage of images and sounds, where dialogue does not find its meaning.

Cyclic type in that human society is built throughout history, another important element through which we are interconnected, is very well pointed out by the directors mentioned. For example, in the film Koyaanisqatsi, starting in the 33rd minute, a complex sequence of buildings, bridges, and streets in an advanced stage of degradation are demolished to make way for new glass buildings. Similarly, in the movie Samsara we see in the 47th minute a factory of workers assembling various appliances, a sequence followed by a series of new cars that are put on a ship to be delivered for sale, and then we see a center iron recycling where machines and other objects are crushed, destroyed, processed.

4.4. Narrative structure in poetic documentary

Even though many of the poetic films do not follow a classical narrative structure, they have a natural tendency to form certain patterns to convey a message.

Moreover, a very important aspect to mention under the research method used (structural-semiotic analysis) is the connection that the director of poetic documentaries builds with his audience. Mirroring one's vision of the surrounding universe is the foundation behind the narrative structure. The choice of a certain rhythm of colors, of the alternation night-day, life-death, of the contrast between nature and the urbanized society, are subjective elements selected by the author and which give birth to the whole narrative structure.

So in Brakhage's documentary, Window Water Baby Moving, we see a series of detailed plans cut out in quick succession that describe not only the relationship between the two protagonists through their intimate gestures and expressiveness of faces but the chaotic rhythm in which life and emotions unfold. This chaotic rhythm is achieved with the help of dynamic editing and in the movie Samsara, minute 56, when we see groups of people consuming or buying chaotically. In the same disorganized way in the 49th minute of Koyaanisqatsi, the city streets are full of people and cars that disappear and appear from all directions. Chaos is a pulse that absorbs people, cars, buildings: everything to do with us.

In modern documentaries, we notice that the authors choose to gradually introduce us to a new world. For example, in Samsara the 33-minute transition from the exotic, tribal world to the heavily transformed human universe is made through a succession of overall frames with suspended highways on which many cars move. This "ant" of human civilization then becomes more and more visible as the pace begins to accelerate.

The Emperor's March (2005) is a French documentary that presents the habits of penguins during a year: their mating rituals, their migration, laying eggs, searching for food, etc. The film is accompanied by an external voice in the form of a dialogue between two characters (in the original version). Made in French, the dialogue and poetic images create a moderate, relatively constant rhythm throughout the film. Although it is a documentary about nature, we see the authors try a fresh approach to the content. This concept of dialogue gradually introduces us to the world of penguins we discover with great curiosity.

The first images show us a group of penguins walking along the horizon. Just below the disk of fire, they resemble humans - they are described as nomads performing an ancient ritual. Through the images from the film's exhibition, a connection is created between the audience and the penguins. Shortly after this humanized opening, the film establishes (through images, not through scientific explanations) that these impressive nomads are emotional beings who, as individuals, form a society. Individual penguins have separate personalities and desires but subordinate to those in the group, as a whole. The entire action of the film focusing on the phenomenon of reproduction of these creatures, it is the one that sets the tone for all the "actions" that viewers witness. The motivations of penguins are to survive as a group, to reproduce;

If at Stan Brakhage his wife's birth was filmed by hand, in a montage with dense, chaotic cuts, we see that in this situation the approach of the subject was made through long frames, from the tripod, using ambient sounds and fictional dialogue. Thus, it is more and more obvious to us that the method of conceptualizing a subject of the poetic documentary can be very different, compared to the other ways of the documentary.

The visual simplicity of the black and white objects that move, against the endless expansion of ice, sky, and later, water matches the simplicity of the story. These simplicities allow the contouring of the visual landscape and the main narrative thread. There are many obstacles for penguins: pain, conflict, sacrifice, and loss are juxtaposed with moments inspired by humor, redemption, love, beauty, and achievement. The universality of the story allows the viewer to get lost inside the frames to enjoy the beauty of the film and the landscapes and the complete amazement of the fact that this happens on the same Earth as the cinema that gives it life. Also, take care of how an individual feels this unbelievable adventure of a lifetime.

The scientific explanation is not the central point of the narrative (nor does it intend to be so); it is the background for the amazing shape that brings a deep and satisfying story to the viewers.

Nature or natural elements are often presented in static or very slightly panoramic ways. A directorial choice that makes us stop, to "rest" our gaze on these imperishable buildings. Their appearance has a circular role in narrative construction. They often appear after the climax of a certain sequence, reminding us of where we started and where we return.

The subject of the film Samsara is also built in a circular role. The film begins with a few Buddhist temples in Myanmar and ends with the call of the monks and the destruction of the newly built mandala, the construction of which was presented in the film's exhibition.

Baraka begins with a few frames of nature that continue with other images from a Buddhist temple, the end of the film being built in the first phase of frames depicting the interior of a church in Jerusalem, and then the film ends well with timelapse nature images. Koyaanisqatsi ends with a frame similar to the one with which it begins, namely an image with cave paintings. The list goes on.

The narrative structure of the poetic documentary does not follow a cognitive-logical line. It is built around emotions that oscillate from the highest peaks to the deepest precipices, so that the spectator is always in a continuous emotional path, in a continuous search. This emotional connection is formed based on the relationship established by the humanized symbols and elements as we observed above. For the whole narrative construction process to work, it is always calibrated so that the viewers do not remain only in a certain palette of emotions, until the end of the film.

4.5. Timing and time

In the film Chronos, as the title points out, the emphasis is mainly on timing and rhythm. We have accelerations of cinematic time through timelapse, but also movements made in slow motion, as the comparative study shows, which support the concept of relativity of human experiences in relation to time, a phenomenon discovered in more recent films by the same authors. Given that the entire film Chronos focuses on the history of human civilization, by making a montage with the most important buildings left standing, time itself acquires a symbolic value that transcends the linear concept of "historical time".

An eloquent example of this kind of film is the 70-minute excerpt from Koyaanisqatsi in which we observe how cinematic time is far from being defined by conventional norms. We have people, crowds of people "flowing" in all directions, while other characters remain stuck in time. This temporal transcendence is a common phenomenon in Ron Fricke's cinematography and associates the concept of time with the different rhythms that each of us chooses to live.

A similar situation can be observed by analyzing a sequence from the documentary Ashes and Snow in which a group of monks enters a temple while a child stays outside and meditates, achieving the same transcendence as in the passage underlined above. We notice that, although the director and the directorial concept differ, otherwise, as a whole, certain similarities stand out.

During the same film, "awakening to life" takes place. The film starts in slow-motion images, and the editing pace will be accentuated along the way, the cinematic time reaching fast forward, timelapse, towards the end of the film.

Ron Fricke describes our timing as a true place of worship, in which our ability to separate the evil from good, ugly from beauty, forces us to ignore the cinematic functions of rhythm and to take the material as a unitary whole, in which the most important aspect remains the audiovisual fluency. We can observe a correlation between the circular construction with a slow beginning, a crescendo, and a descrescendo, starting and ending in the same narrative rhythm in all the films of these authors.

The passage of time is also underlined by the day-night or new-old alternation, meticulously constructed during the films we comment on here. Returning to the abyss of human roots, in the barren lands of the deserts or high forests of the Amazon, helps us to contemplate the existence of time itself and what it means for us who are limited by its peculiarities. Ron Fricke argues, also in the interview for The Lip, that time is more than a support for flow and interconnections, it is the interconnection itself in which human remains captive. Returning to the sphere of temporality, we discover, therefore, that our daily space, life, but also our dreams are processed in a common vision governed by the unwritten laws of time.

In Regen (1929), these aesthetic properties are reflected in the construction and creativity of the film. To observe how time plays an important role in the film's construction, I propose to remember a little of the action, or what we could call it, in the absence of a more appropriate term. In the first part, the spectator is presented with a situation: Amsterdam, its roofs, its canals, and, incidentally, its inhabitants. Then the spectator is slowly introduced to the event: the raindrops send tiny waves through a canal, a breeze blows, the birds fly. The rain is falling harder and we are getting closer to the characters who are adapting to the changing environment. Their faces are mostly anonymous - they appear quickly and mix in the crowd when the umbrellas are raised. As the streets clear, the focus is on the interaction of rain with nature and architecture - filling dams, flowing through sewer pipes, etc. And finally, we return to the status quo: although there is evidence of the storm - the streets are still silver and water droplets can be seen on the railings - the canals have turned into a glassy calm and people are coming out from inside. Amsterdam is vibrant once again. The documentary was filmed for months, synchronizing various specific aspects of the city during the rain. Amsterdam is vibrant once again. The documentary was filmed for months, synchronizing various specific aspects of the city during the rain. Amsterdam is vibrant once again. The documentary was filmed for months, synchronizing various specific aspects of the city during the rain.

By manipulating time we are made to feel that everything happens during an afternoon. The condensation of real-time into cinematic time is the process behind this documentary (and not just his). This aspect thus demonstrates, once again, the subjective dimension that poetic documentaries assume.

4.6. Sound and music

The documentaries made by Fricke and Magidson are the most conclusive example of the construction of audiovisual aesthetics. Because they do not exploit verbal language as a form of audiovisual communication, the stylistics of the whole concept focus on the musicality of natural sounds or the music itself. We can see how in Chronos the sound of the bell is used as a specific atmosphere for the cathedral interiors whose images are present, thus highlighting both the spatial musicality and the symbolism of this element represented by the call to spirituality.

The ability of images to guide the viewer throughout the artistic concept, without any help of verbal arguments, explains the degree of maturity shown by the creators of poetic documentaries in an attempt to use the image as visual support for philosophical thinking, a fact noted and by Walter Addiego and mentioned in the San Francisco Chronicle article: "The Samsara Documentary is a Charming Visual Experience" is not a message in words - the film has no dialogue or narrative - but it is distinguished by the energy and force of clarity "(Addiego).

Starting from the transmission of the consubstantial message to the film, we notice that it is in close connection with the music and ambient sounds used. Each image has its personality due to the soundtrack running simultaneously. Moreover, the polarity of the environment in which the action takes place stimulates the viewer towards an active connection with the atmosphere of the world described in the film.

Another form of construction of poetic sequences stands out during the documentary Ashes and Snow by introducing philosophical monologues that aim to articulate the visual message. Surgically mounted images turn into a matrix of the message underlined by words. We have, therefore, not only ambient sounds or music, but also poetry or philosophical texts present throughout the poetic documentaries, which support not only the lack of a traditional rhythm and time but also a recurrence of the inner voice of the creator.

Ambient sounds, most of the time, converge in an ensemble that gives us a state of uncertainty. The viewer fails to realize whether the sound he is receiving is a natural ambient sound or is just a sound effect meant to create a connection between the atmosphere in the images and the music on the soundtrack. An example would be the desert sequence present in the film Chronos, more precisely at the minute 8:30, when the experimental sound in the background is confused bizarrely with the wind sound specific to the local geography.

A new controversial situation appears in the film Baraka in the 63rd minute, when several workers shovel a solid material into the furnaces. The sonic ambiance reproduces a sound of flames that mastered gains another stylistic value.

Music, for the most part, is present in the form of a sound experiment. Composer Michael Stearns, combining experimental music with processed or natural ambient sounds, manages to aurally construct the state needed for audiovisual ambivalence to be fully exploited.

As I pointed out earlier, in the poetic documentaries made by Deren and Brakhage the soundtrack is missing, but its lack has a strong aesthetic impact on the audience. The viewer is forced to channel his attention to the images, not being distracted by other external stimuli. The lack of sound not only forces us to focus on form as a whole but also stimulates our subjectivity, each of us being forced to fill the gap left by the lack of soundtrack with sounds or other elements of personal experience, stored in emotional memory. Many scenes in the films of the two authors are strongly loaded with sound stimuli (faces crying, laughing, giggling, moving water, etc.), so avoiding a confrontation with the lack of soundtrack is impossible.

In the Qatsi series, the soundtrack is exploited to amplify the semiotics of the images. If in Brakhage the films were designed and could work independently of the sound, in Godfrey Reggio this can no longer be done. When the volume of the soundtrack is reduced to a minimum, the images lose their rhythm and often their meaning.

A major difference can be noticed between the concepts of the documentary in terms of soundtrack. We see how sound and music are often used to support the image, but most of the time the sound remains in the artificial sphere, it is not integrated to reproduce reality. Even if some of the poetic documentaries also use natural sounds, they are used exclusively to suggest the existence of symbols or to maintain a certain emotional state, to the detriment of reproducing a real situation.

4.7. Image

Looking closer at the intrinsic universe of the works we are referring to, we see the visual resemblance between the films of the great cinematic revolutions, such as The Man with the Camera, Regen, and Ron Fricke's films.

Separated from almost a century of existence, recent films seem to exhaustively use many of the techniques discovered and used by the fathers of cinema in their films that dealt with various subjects from a poetic perspective. This shows to us the universality of aesthetics in relation to the object, but also special rhythmicity that only a non-verbal film could manage with such mastery. Special attention paid to aesthetics reveals the authors' preference for the subliminal message behind the mounting mechanism.

Proportion is seen by the authors of the poetic mode as the main element in the construction of images. The way to use equal, unequal proportions, to balance the visual compositions, or to transform them into dynamic, fluid images is as if inspired by Policlet's treatise that I mentioned in one of the subchapters of this paper (1.1.). Following certain precise mathematical principles, the beautiful or the grotesque manage not only to contrast in juxtaposed images but also to complement each other. If Policlet explains in his work that perfection is achieved by precise proportions, and these proportions are the median result of the sum of the forms of that category, both Fricke and the other modern authors do not discount this rule.

Aesthetics is also exploited through the naturalness of costumes or body paintings practiced in different cultures. Thus, we discover in the film Baraka the indescribable beauty of the aborigines, with their bodies adorned with necklaces, bracelets, and various small accessories faces painted in countless patterns, built of dots. This phenomenon is observed throughout the film, in the Amazons where the scarlet paint shines on the forehead of a young woman looking through the green leaves of a tree. Addressing the theme of body painting is a direct way to communicate our return to the primordial aesthetics of man and his primary sense of aesthetics.

I had previously discussed what Mark Magidson defined as flow, or rather, that kind of connection between passages that leads the visual thread from one image to another: "[Samsara] is about flow and the interconnection between things. I could only see this during editing, editing the film without music or sound. We made small content groups and then let the images guide us "(Silva). From this context, we understand the position that the creator adopts in relation to his work. Above a simple "spiritual journey" as Mark Magidson wants to call it, the world that arises from the flow of images becomes an original world, a world in which the paradigms of contemporary society intertwined with the past, present and future.

We have the honor of knowing the intimacy of a space whose perspective exhibits the naturalness of the world and the artistic spirit. Beauty is born from empathy for the visual composition of the director, in which the rules are not used only for aesthetic purposes; they pass beyond the stereotypical naturalness of nature, leading us into a world of the poetic, of reflection. As we discussed in Chapter 1, page 14, the paradigm of beauty changes according to social and cultural transformations. Even at the level of contemporary society, beauty is treated according to the perishable cultural trends of the times we live in.

But what even the poetic documentaries point out is that model of beauty that does not lose its meaning. The classical forms, and the forms coming from the popular culture in the poetic documentaries, have a static character, well exposed in the structure of the films.

Color plays an essential role in the semiotics of the audiovisual language. Besides its technical role, color induces the viewer to certain states depending on the code of the cultural paradigm in which it ends up being exploited. For ordinary viewers, devoid of cinematic culture, the story is the most important element of any film. The color of an icon can have a major impact on maintaining the viewer's attention and supporting the story. For example, when a frame changes from a warm-yellow sensation to a cold-blue sensation in successive images, it can be quite difficult for the viewer's attention to the film is maintained. Here, color correction helps the quality of the final version. Color correction helps to standardize the color recorded during the production stage, and to give a more relevant image, allowing the viewer to focus on the story.

The most common colors have a standard social meaning, while specific colors could contextualize a particular mood or personal idea. These meanings often do not go beyond the limits of the society that has given colors a certain meaning. An example is a color (non-color) black, which often represents death in Western society, while white is used to symbolize death in Eastern cultures (Faur).

We notice special attention that documentarians pay to colors in the construction of poetic documentaries. The predominant colors are green and blue, which are the basic colors in nature (life is built around them).

A concrete example of the strongly semantically connoted use of colors can be seen throughout the Naqoyqatsi documentary where color becomes the mainstay in narrative construction. Experimentally, the filmmakers chose a certain color to represent the states and actions described in the images. We have, in the example above, the image of members of the Ku Klux Klan over which a red filter was applied, thus suggesting the concept of bloody violence.

The poverty of the working class and those in developing countries are carefully portrayed in gray, colored grays, and unsaturated tones. This way of presenting reality has the effect of generalizing the current situation in the areas that are the subject of the documentaries. Because the film cannot essentially capture the whole atmosphere (nor does it want to), the message or content is idealized, propagandistic, similar to that of the propaganda documentaries presented in Subchapter 2.2.

The meanings constructed by the set of lines, points, and spots are defined in relation to the applied aesthetics. Each society and culture is shaped by a specific paradigm of aesthetics in general. The lines, in the proper sense, do not exist in nature, nor do the dots or spots. They appear in the form of optical phenomena that occur when the group of objects moves away from the viewer.

Another semiotic use of the line, this time also inside the Naqoyqatsi documentary, can be seen at minute 8 when the image of people is overexposed with the image of lines similar to barcodes, thus suggesting the concept of transforming people into products, which can be sold in supermarkets.

Great emphasis is placed on the contour light, emphasizing the shapes and movements in the decor. In addition to the role of ambiance, light thus acquires a dramatic function supported by the set of lines and the increasing rhythm.

The author then introduces us to the metropolitan area of an unspecified city, respecting the same rhythm, the same chromatic and dynamic. Another important aspect is the excessive use of primary geometric shapes, straight lines, and trajectory movements, thus structuring a very safe and very rhythmic mechanism of the audiovisual message. In addition to this geometrical consistency, this whole set of primary compositional elements reminds us of the art of Antiquity, but also of the construction of archetypal forms that carry a universal message in relation to the entire documentary.

Regardless of the media format, we are referring to, it will include text as a medium for transmitting the information. So, we notice how this important visual symbol in our culture is carefully selected in various contexts throughout the poetic documentaries, to support the image.

One of the concrete examples appears in the 68th minute of the film Powaqqatsi when on a wall is written in red paint "guerrilla warfare", and a girl with a red box in her hand stops near the wall looking at the room. The author shows us in this way the struggle between the future of the next generations and the present, by using a text with strong signaling and premonitory value.

Another conclusive example can be seen in Samsara, at minute 80, where we are presented with an image with the wall between Palestine and Israel on which he writes suggestively: "I want my ball back!", Later being added "thanks!", Suggesting thus the rupture between normality and reality.

As mentioned earlier, movement as an aesthetic element in all arts visually is one of the most important general characteristics, whether we refer to the movement of the video camera in the audiovisual or to the movement suggested by the lines of perspectives and shapes.

Moving shapes are often visually coordinated to describe the relationships between various elements and to form coherent ensembles. The relationship between nature and man is often depicted in moving shapes. One of the most representative examples appears in the documentary Powaqqatsi, minute 17, where we see a natural waterfall which then, by enlarging the frame with the help of the zoom-out effect, turns into an artificially formed waterfall by manipulating the watercourse by man.

The slow motion effect is intensely used in all modern poetic documentaries. Using this effect, documentarians manage to show us another facet of the surrounding world that we usually miss because of the amalgam of visual stimuli that manifests around us. But in Ashes and Snow, the slow motion effect is applied to sequences that transcend cinematic space and time. From the first minute of the film, an external voice superimposed on images filmed in slow motion tells us "If you come to me at this moment, your minutes will become hours, your hours will become days and your days will become a lifetime." Thus, the dilation of time is achieved not only through this technological process, but also through the narrative argument that leads us, as an illusionist, into timeless and spatial.

It could confuse and it could be considered that the film Ashes and Snow would strictly respect the characteristics of the visual essay because of the text which is, mostly, a philosophical, poetic, abstract one, but also because of the approached theme, namely: spiritual development of man with nature. But the film, as we can see, uses actual images to represent reality (mostly), whether we are talking about the meditation of monks or the animal world. Besides this aspect, the subject approached is as tangible as possible, real., an expository, observational, or performative documentary can be made on the same topic (of man's connection with nature).

In another eloquent example, in La Marche de L'empereur, right at the end of the film (minute 78), it is a seven-shot in slow motion that represents when the penguin cubs enter the water for the first time. Although the film does not include any other sequence filmed by this technical process, the author opts to slow down the image to generate a feeling of joy springing from the pleasure of small swimmers. The joy of meeting penguins with water is not only prolonged by the slow motion effect but gains another meaning: from ephemeral, simple joviality, it turns into the crucial moment in the life of those animals. This moment becomes, practically, a ritual, a transition to maturity.

Camera movements are used to describe spaces, actions, follow characters, and generate emotions. These are classified, according to the directions of the geared dynamics, into several categories. During the poetic documentaries, we observe the entire range of camera movements. From descriptive or follow-up panoramas to helicopter or underwater camera footage (as in Ashes and Snow), poetic documentary filmmakers try to use every means of filming to capture - with as strong a visual impact as possible. on the spectators - the situations presented in the film. The visual counts and speaks its word through itself, through its radiating force. Even "hand-held" filming is not avoided, the aesthetics of this style of filming being intensely exploited,

Rhythm is used in audiovisual products to construct drama or stress certain states or ideas. It is usually built on music, the images being cropped exactly when the sound resumes a passage or changes. Perhaps the most spectacular way in which the rhyme is used in the film is found in this mode of the documentary. We can observe the rhythm of military choreographies, religious meetings, traditional customs (as in Powaqqatsi, minute 44), the rhythm of natural elements, buildings, cities, lights, but the most obvious and prominent rhythm remains the rhythm of digital elements. If the other forms of rhythm in the image are integrated into the universal ensemble, more or less, these rhythms formed by digital codes or digital visual experiments, through various overlaps or digital processing, have a separate aesthetic.

Regarding the aesthetics of the human face, the authors of all modern poetic documentaries use it as a leitmotif faces belonging to various cultures. The figures of the people remain fixed, staring at the room nailed or remain trapped in slow motion, lost in a vast metropolitan space. We often see the faces of robots doing the same or the faces of silicone dolls. Through this strategy, the authors not only make us pay attention, we notice certain similarities and differences between cultures or between people and artificial forms, but also have as a fundamental purpose to present the adaptation of man to modern social life and the way they relate to this adaptation, in contrast to the expressiveness that the world manifests.

Contrast is no less used than other expressive features of the elements of plastic language. For example, during the film La Marche de L'empereur (the version narrated by Morgan Freeman), more precisely at minute 18, there is a sequence in which the sky, captured at sunset, acquires shades of red, in contrast to the landscape below the line. the horizon is presented in shades of blue-gray. We have in this sequence not only a contrast of the primary or warm-cold colors, but also a contrast used for semiotic purposes: the sunset of the quiet, abundant period, and the brutal arrival of winter.

The visual world of poetic documentaries represents the central point around which it agglutinates the whole narrative structure. Its importance is given by the ability of the image to generate strong emotions that the public easily receives. The image of frozen penguins in Antarctica or the image of a religious ritual can sensitize the public in the directions desired by the director, and this phenomenon is largely due to the use of a universal visual language and an aesthetic that also tends - all powers - to a certain universality.

5. Poetic documentary and future film trends

The poetic documentary, however, does not stop only at the elements mentioned in the previous chapters and subchapters. Even if the content and technique he uses has more or less approached reality (through a subjective approach), we have various examples of poetic documentaries that can also exist in a hybrid format, at the intersection of documentary film modes.

The emancipation tendencies of the documentary, at the beginning of the internet era in the '90s, were centered around the interaction between the public and this new technology that would completely change the paradigm of the relationship between people and cultural products. The public becomes aware of the freedom in the selection of content and distribution platforms so that the way the public will choose media content will be completely different from the period before the Internet. Websites dedicated to virtual reviews, such as imdb.com or rottentomatoes.com, filters and provides a wide range of information about the documentaries we want to watch. Distribution platforms offer the ability to view documentaries anytime and anywhere via Internet-connected devices.

Even for poetic documentary filmmakers, access to a wide range of stock images, free online courses, or advanced technical means offered by video processing programs, all in terms of home comfort, has meant a radical change in the way they relate. to the whole process of producing and distributing a film.

The ingenuity of the creators of the poetic documentary film was not limited to the language and characteristics of classical cinema, they constantly trying to adapt to new requirements and trends. Faced with the absence of the necessary archive footage and the relative lack of official documents, Rithy Panh had to look for replacement elements in the making of the film entitled The Missing Picture (2013). He came to use clay figurines, placed in dioramas, images mixed and superimposed with the few existing archive materials, along with songs and speeches of the Khmer Rouge organization, followers of the Communists in Kampuchea, the party that dominated Cambodia in 1975-1979. "I don't care much when I start a film if it's going to be a documentary or a fiction,"

The Missing Picture is the example that can demonstrate the connection between the poetic and the expository mode (for example), but also the connection between documentary, fiction, and other ways of approaching a story.

The image from modern poetic documentaries (which we discussed during Chapter 4) is the dominant element, through which, directly, the content will be constructed and delivered to the viewer, in the background dominating the film music. But in this kind of hybrid documentary, the image plays an equal role with the sound, so the sound draws a clear ideational outline in the construction of the film.

The subjective experience, constructed and illustrated by a unique, personalized concept (specific to the poetic documentary), is meant to complete the soundtrack made up of the external voice and many other kinds of overlapping sounds. The poetic documentary is thus detached from its classical period in which minimalist themes were treated visually as personal experiences, the modern period where the subject overcomes minimalist barriers and builds an overview of contemporary society, reaching an atypical approach to any type of subject (be it minimalist or macrosocial) - through concrete images, digitally constructed images, symbolic images, archive images, photographs, paintings, figurines, external voice, poems, ambient sounds, archive sounds, experimental sounds, etc.

What is the current poetic documentary and what will be in the future through this immersive approach depends very much on how the authors relate to the content and its form. Thus, we see a series of documentaries in a hybrid format (either between documentary and fiction or between documentary and other audiovisual products) that implement some specific characteristics of the poetic documentary. From narrated poems, visual illustrations specific to certain moods, content elements defined poetically, a whole series of documentaries have emerged as a direct response to technological transformations (the same type of transformation that occurs periodically throughout history).

Documentary film has practically become a new fad. However, the most important documentary film productions in recent years have been films made for classical television, on the horizon of traditional forms of production and distribution. The new era of the film has not (yet) managed to become the dominant paradigm.

We live, however, in a favorable period, in which the production of documentary film has known a large scale: recording with digital cameras and mobile phones, editing with programs such as Premiere, Final Cut or iMovie, funding through networking funds and distribution through platforms such as YouTube or Vimeo. Also, there are various platforms (some available free of charge) for the exclusive distribution of documentaries (as mentioned at the end of Chapter 1). In the digital environment, the number of documentaries and audiovisual materials made available to the public has increased exponentially. The existing archives and the collaborative style, developed through the Internet, made it possible to access many television and film documentaries, from the commercial circuit and from outside it.

When Flaherty made the film Nanook from the North, the technical equipment needed for filming and editing was very expensive, and the whole process was slow and cumbersome. When Rouch and Morin filmed The Chronicle of a Veri, they had lighter and cheaper cameras, and the technology for capturing synchronized sounds was already available. The technique determines what we mean by reality and the type of reality that can be effectively documented and displayed in documentaries. For example, the story in Tarnation (2003) would have been impossible to document when Buñuel filmed Las Hurdes (1933). Beyond the tragic story described, Tarnation is also the story of the democratization of what can be called "show technology". It is the story of the digital man and the massive transformation of the middle class by creating raw documentary material about their own lives. The point on this journey of cinema was the very ability of the general public to broadcast their content through the Internet.

Nowadays, smartphones and similar devices have radically changed the relationship between individuals and the world around them. They have become the most widely used devices for capturing and playing audiovisual material, every day, for millions of people, becoming the main generators of documentary material on a global scale. As we already know, there are documentaries totally or partially recorded with mobile phones, documentary film festivals, and cinema networks that are increasingly incorporating these formats in their programs.

Reality is also forced to define itself through editing and narration, by combining fragments from different sources. This incisive assembly of fragments was called "creativity" by the Belgian theorist Abraham Moles (Moles). This is why Grierson rightly defined the documentary as "the treatment creative of reality".

5.1. The concepts of cloud filmmaking and VR from the perspective of poetic documentaries

The strategies and styles implemented in the documentaries, as in the case of those in the fiction film, are constantly changing - they have a history - and have changed for various reasons: the dominant modes of the exhibition have changed their discourse. ; the ideological arena of appeals on the issues addressed has also changed. The comfortable way of accepting a certain form of representation of the reality of one generation becomes, for the next generation, an artificial one. New strategies must always be developed to represent "things as they are" and others, innovators, to challenge this representation, later ("The Voice of Documentary").

Digital technology, often perceived as an evolution in the way it is represented in documentaries, has played a significant role in the subsequent formulation of new aesthetic reasons. He achieved this by cultivating a realistic style, filmed through amateur cameras, using the immediate intimacy of technology, based on the digital aspect in its various connotations of authenticity and credibility (Landesman).

One of the most avant-garde concepts at the moment in terms of documentary film is the concept of cloud filmmaking. In an interview with

Tribeca Film Festival for the event's official website, Tiffany Shlain talks about cloud sourcing and returning to the era of collaboration:

"When YouTube first appeared, I had a dream that all the videos would have HD quality and menus that would explain to me how I could get the copyright. I was like a child in a candy store ... this explosion of online video was not only a much bigger candy store than I ever dreamed of, but it completely changed the way I make movies. The new tools and technologies that allow video sharing have allowed me and my team at The Moxie Institute to embark on a new adventure that we call cloud filmmaking. "

(Shlain)

What is this new concept of making the documentary film we discover on the official website: letitripple.org. The mission of this project is to use films, technology, discussion materials, and events to engage the 21st-century audience in conversation and action around the complicated topics that shape our lives, as described on the website. This concept goes beyond what Riddley Scott did through the Life in a Day project (2011). If in Life in a Day the spectator also became part of the story, in the vision of Let It Tripple the spectator does not only become part of the story, but the whole project is realized through the spectator.

The documentary is not limited to the final audiovisual material, the documentary is now the whole process of pre-production, production, and post-production, also a process of debates, attitudes, and actions that process energy and information from a global environment, from a global team, on global issues (and not only). Thus, we see that the voice of the common consciousness, which Fricke or Magidson promoted through modern poetic documentaries, becomes the main engine in the elaboration of new concepts of documentary film. The interconnection we discussed in the previous chapter culminates in the history of the genre. To understand the magnitude of this new global phenomenon we must quote a few lines from the official website:

"In the last ten years we have created and distributed 31 films, engaging over 50 million people in dialogue, we have initiated a new way of making films called" cloud filmmaking "collaborating with people around the world, we have found a new model for global conversations with screenings and discussions on all continents on the same day, with a combination of live and virtual events. The Let It Ripple team initiated the global days of the film and discussions about important issues that shape our lives by uniting over 130,000 live events related together with moderators and common themes. It has grown from 1,500 events in the first year to over 133,000 events in 125 countries. " (Www.letitripple.org)

On the other hand, new technology is appearing on the market and entering our lives faster and deeper. If in recent years we have been able to experience VR (Virtual Reality) technology at film festivals or through electronics stores, today the VR world has become a relatively tangible element for the general public.

Using mobile phones together with VR Box support, we can watch movies made at 360 degrees, we can test games on video consoles or PCs. It publishes a multitude of documentaries made by National Geographic and other major documentary filmmakers for free on the Youtube platform and uses VR technology. Two decades ago, cheap digital cameras changed the documentary landscape with possibilities such as low light filming, hiding cameras, and recording in any conditions. Not to mention the democratization of documentary film. Today, VR is ready to make a quantum leap, giving viewers an extremely intense, visceral experience of being in another world. As we might expect, VR is currently expensive in terms of the recording and editing process (compared to the production process of a classic documentary). In the meantime, cameras have appeared for ordinary users, at modest prices, but which do not yet offer a superior image quality.

The VR world is in its infancy, and for this way of telling stories to be truly adopted by the public, as it was at the beginning of classical cinema, it will have to develop a particular cinematic language. Being able to see and film in 360 degrees, the cinematic paradigm transforms. Of note is how the documentary film explores this new technology or another way of collaborating called cloud filmmaking. What will be the poetic documentary, concerning the innovations presented briefly, remains to be seen, but we can see that the poetic documentary also exists in the era of cloud filmmaking and VR. In Life in a Day, at minute 15, we have an excerpt edited using rhythm and directorial concept elements specific to the poetic documentary (discussed in the previous chapter).

5.1.1. Movie review: Waves of Grace

One of the VR films made poetically that caught my attention is the movie Waves of Grace (2015). It is a film with a topical story: a look through the eyes of a survivor of the Ebola epidemic in Liberia, named Deconte Davis. She was infected with Ebola, but survived and is now one of the few people who can interact freely with patients because there is no chance she can contract the disease again. This is a gift and a curse to her - she can soothe the dying, but she can't do anything for most of them.

With a difficult subject to following, the most terrible scenes are set in a cemetery, as people in white costumes specific to catastrophes lay dozens of corpses. The external voice present over the film's images is thought of as a prayer addressed to the divinity in which she, the narrator, apologizes for not being able to do more in this fight against the disease and asks for her help. The images we see throughout the film are images that, most of the time, have nothing to do with the external voice or the theme of the film. Groups of children running through garbage, through gangs, through the schoolyard, people walking quietly in the urban agglomeration of underdeveloped cities, make up most of the scenes. We observe, thus, that the author intends to visually describe an atmosphere to us,

Connecting frames, camera movements, types of plans, perspectives, are lost in the universe of 360 ° images. The camera becomes a man, a typical observer, engaged in the middle of the story with the freedom and autonomy that he did not have until now. We must also not ignore the position of the camera in space. The room often places us in the middle of the crowd, whether it is part of the class of students, cemetery, or hospital. The people in the film look at us, address us, interact socially with us, which makes Waves of Grace an immersive experience in the true sense of the word. The line between reality and technology becomes almost imperceptible.

Although this technology allows us to experience a space or a situation in an original and complex way, it comes with its limitations. In the construction of the sequences from Waves of Grace, the action takes place at a slow pace, close to observational, so that the sequences give us the necessary time to be able to go through and analyze the entire 360 ° plane. But if we wanted a dynamic montage obtained by accelerating the cinematic time, as in Baraka (1992), minute 48, our ability to process the images unfolded at an accelerated pace, in 360 °, or with a cut out every few seconds is limited. Thus, the reception of the message will be difficult.

Waves of Grace gives us that immersive experience that our expectations anticipate from a product that uses VR technology. The limits of technology and human senses, however, make VR a model that, at least for now, follows a strict set of rules in video production, such as long sequence shots, cinematic time played at real speed or even in slow motion, medium intensity actions.

Of course, visual experiments can be performed that do not follow these rules, but in terms of VR documentary, the introduction of such frames will make it even more difficult to receive the message already loaded with information, by the very nature of the genre.

5.2. Interactive documentaries and their connection with the aesthetics of the poetic mode

Although nonlinear forms of film narration are a relatively recent phenomenon, they are less researched, and their description can be a problem because the field is developing and in a permanent transition. Also, hardware and software are constantly changing, so that more interactive multimedia work can no longer be viewed due to changes in distribution platforms. When conservation practices have not been applied, the works of art remain invisible, unavailable. About newer projects, such as interactive documentaries on the internet, where both content and appearance are new, it is too early to conclude media opportunities and future development scenarios.

The fundamental difference between a linear and an interactive documentary is not the transition from analog to digital technology, but the transition from a linear story to an interactive narrative. Both linear and interactive documentaries try to create a dialogue with reality. If the viewing of a linear documentary requires cognitive participation of the spectators (the act of interpretation), the interactive documentary requires physical participation, the decisions translate into a physical act, such as clicks, moving, speaking, etc. (Gaudenzi 26).

In interactive-participatory documentaries, where user-generated content can be used to populate a web documentary, this responsibility is diluted and sometimes impossible to follow (Gaudenzi 34). When the author is responsible for an interactive structure (for example, a website), but not for the content that populates it, the question may arise as to what happens to the author's intent and who will be held responsible for the documentary's message. The notion of the director as the main performer thus becomes a difficult subject to define (Gaudenzi 34-35).

Considering the "interactive" and "participatory" character of the spectator, we conclude that considering alternatives is a natural way of thinking, not only in terms of planning life and actions but also in terms of works of art. That consideration is an important part of everyday life and decision-making. As a result, non-linear, interactive works of art (as well as games and other forms of culture and entertainment), where different possibilities and "lives" can be tried, are an interesting environment for spectators and especially for artists who design games. Such a person is like an archetypal storyteller who creates a perfect narrative world that can be experienced in many ways.

Nichols' ways of defining and classifying documentaries remain as introductory landmarks at the intersection of advanced internet technology and cloud filmmaking. Thus, the author of The Living Documentary, Sandra Gaudenzi, after long analyzes of the 15 years of activity as a TV producer, develops a classification of documentaries according to the basic interaction between these interactive documentaries and user-viewers.

These new self-reflective documentaries mix observational passages with interviews, the external voice with intertexts, outlining what was obvious at all times: documentaries have always been forms of representation, never clear windows to "reality"; the filmmaker has always been a participant-witness and an active constructor of meaning, a producer of cinematic discourse, rather than a neutral reporter or a total connoisseur of documented phenomena ("The Voice of Documentary").

But before we delve very deeply into this issue, I would like to analyze an efficient and coherent way of structuring the methods of classification and reporting to the narrative construction of documentaries, interaction, and roles between creator and user, developed by Anna Wiehl in his work: Interactive Documentaries. Modes of interaction as a crucial factor for the expansion of cognitive experience to physical, emotional, and social engagement (2015). It also makes a brief relevant description of how the whole interaction is developed:

"First of all, by amplifying the complexity of the product, the possibilities of interaction (social), and the spectrum of different functions (which the user assumes), the degree of participation increases. Secondly, the increased degree of participation causes a decrease in the role of the author and the user who become inter-actors, collaborators, and co-creators. Third, amplifying the possibilities for interaction and participation stimulates the expansion of a "documentary experience"cognitive primarily about physical, emotional, and social engagement."

(Wiehl 5)

5.2.1. **Conversational mode**

We thus treat the conversational mode as the first mode described in The Living Documentary. If in this paper the author refers to the conversational interactivity of video games, emphasizing the hybridization between video games and documentaries, she also explains, a little later, that this mode does not necessarily have to be a hybrid between a video game and documentary, but it can even be a digital program that has only the logic of a game (through hyperlink techniques, simulation of reality, the logic of experience, etc.). The fundamental connection between this mode of narrative construction and the poetic documentary is realized through the subjective character of the experience lived by the spectator. If in the first poetic documentaries, analyzed throughout the work,

Taken as an example, a classic documentary (the expository mode, see subchapter 3.2.) Has in its structure a whole suite of specific information and data. It is categorically made to deliver this information to the spectators in a unidirectional, objective way. The form is generally treated and elaborated in a structured way, most often following the chronology of events or a logical thread of the concept. How far goes with transforming the documentary into these new digital environments, explains Sandra Gaudenzi:

"In 2002, the use of artificial intelligence to build realistic worlds was applied to a game launched on the Internet by the US military called the US Army. The intention was to give civilians a perspective on the life of a soldier from the barracks to the battlefields. The game, says filmmaker Randy Horton, was "designed, produced and distributed entirely as a documentary project.", and military personnel test and provide feedback during the game to ensure the authenticity of this experience."

(Gaudenzi 43; Horton 5)

The conversational mode is not limited to simulating experiences through play to develop new skills and knowledge. This way can be approached and integrated into immersive journalism. This is a form of journalism that allows the viewer to watch the events in the middle of the action, in news and documentaries. Using 3D games and immersive technologies that create a sense of "being there" and provide the opportunity to get personally involved in a story, immersive journalism places a member of the public directly in the event allowing them to interact in real-time with the facts. and the elements present.

By accessing a virtual version of where the story takes place, as a witness/participant or experiencing the perspective of a character described in the news story, the audience could gain unprecedented access to the attractions and sounds and even feelings and emotions that accompany the news (From Peña, Weil, and Llobera).

However, the difference between immersive non-fiction and documentary games is more difficult to define, especially since there is not yet a body of research to help determine what news games are in relation to documentary games. In Tracy Fullerton's article on documentary games, she provides some such examples that recreate the events in Pearl Harbor or allow a user to participate in a re-enactment of the Iraq war scenario in which Hussein's sons were killed or play the role. a victim of the September 11 attack (Fullerton).

Probably the key to clarifying the difference would be that immersive journalism uses an experience embodied in an unchanged narrative, which allows questions about the environment without changing the trajectory of each individual. It more closely reflects a traditional journalistic or documentary practice. Consider the IPSRESS project which uses a technical unit through which individuals have been placed in a virtual body of a detainee in a stressful position (De la Peña, "Towards Immersive Journalism: The IPSRESS Experience").

One person in this experiment listened to an audio file with the true transcript of Mohammed al-Qahtani's interrogation, read by the actors as if they were coming from another room. This was a recreation of a real event and the experience proved to be authentic from a journalistic point of view. After this immersive experience was completed, the British government released a video associated with the trial of the death of the civilian Baha Mousa. The video released helped establish the veracity of this special construct of immersive journalism, which was based on the reports of the Freedom of Information Act and the international descriptions of the Red Cross.

The examples presented show us how poetic documentary not only manages to continue as a documentary film but also becomes an important source to be exploited in the process of switching to new technologies. The emphasis is on in the immersive documentaries on the lived experience, on emotions, it also represents the fundamental characteristic that we encounter in the structure of the classic poetic documentaries.

Our transposition, as spectators, even in a virtual world, proposes an active approach to the subject that can certainly be more interactive and can take you out of the comfort of passive watching on a couch. The main problem of interactive media, in a particular conversational mode, is the willingness of viewers to become active and participate directly in the dynamics of such material, requiring significant resources of energy and concentration. These materials are generally dedicated to a mature audience with superior analysis-synthesis capacity.

5.2.2. Hypertext mode

Another way described by Sandra Gaudenzi is the hypertext mode which refers to the possibility that by accessing a graphical interface and interacting with it through various commands, the viewer can choose the materials he wants to watch or with which he wants to interact.

The conversational mode is differentiated from the hypertext mode to create a type of fluid and receptive interaction between the user and the technology used. This form of interaction is referred to as a type of "conversation" regarding the spontaneity and connectivity obtained between the user and the device. On the contrary, according to Gaudenzi (2013), the hypertext mode, which appeared on personal computers in the Apple Multimedia Lab in the late 1980s ("Interactive Documentary context", 2015), the interaction was modeled around the algorithmic potential of computers. Although the computational potential of machines is used in both modes, in hypertext mode, the resources of a computer are used to establish in advance a series of fixed links between network nodes.

The hypertext mode was very popular and a multitude of such projects reached the market on different platforms, with a wide range of content and narrative structures. Several production companies are trying to explore ways to give the user some freedom of action, but "its function remains focused on progressing along with a fixed point in the story, and the system remains firmly in control of the narrative trajectory" (Ryan).

Thus, the approach of the content in the mentioned form does not offer documentary filmmakers a vast opportunity to develop poetic documentary projects. The big problem I identified through the analysis of projects like Journey to the End of Coal (2008), The Big Issue: A Web Documentary on the Obesity Epidemic (2009) or Le Grand Incendie (2013) is the discontinuity of the narrative thread, springing from the constant need to interact with the graphical interface (in the current format).

This interaction does nothing but disconnects us from the emotions we experience during a certain sequence, or, as we noted earlier, the experience of emotions and states is the basic element in the poetic documentary. Even if certain hypertext projects meet the other characteristics of the poetic documentary (stated in the previous chapters), forcing the viewer to use this interaction deeply limits the experience of a documentary specific to the poetic mode.

5.2.3. Participatory mode

The spectator's ability to become part of the production, distribution, and review of the podium remains the major asset. Many platforms offer the opportunity to users around the world to take part and to develop common projects through individual contributions. It is almost identical to the previously discussed concept of cloud filmmaking. The major difference is that most platforms (such as Youtube, Vimeo) do not have a restrictive condition regarding the sorting of materials, following some clear aesthetic criteria.

Restricting materials on a particular topic can only be done if they are uploaded to the platform by a single channel, or using a playlist. The material filtering or sorting algorithm is defined by the creators, and the general-purpose remains to cover various categories frequented by users in a single mix, depending on the general preferences of the viewer (depending on what types of materials they watch), over time what cloud filmmaking represents the stages of production and distribution of video materials made by users, respecting the same theme or subject, with a well-established purpose.

An original approach to this mode is the interactive documentary project entitled The Thousandth Tower (2010), which is part of a series (Highrise), starting from the same premise: the stories of some residents of city buildings and the problems they face. If the final interface of the project uses a hypertext logic, in which the user can click only to reveal content, the production process involves an intensive act of participation. Subjects are involved in photographing and taking responsibility for creating a process of change and starting a dialogue with local authorities. Their stories continue, without end, through the steps they take: the official meetings, the decisions taken by the authorities, the community created around the project (Cizek). All this is made public through the interactive platform where users can browse the content. Subjectivity and malleability are high, the characters growing, both mentally and physically, but the images and sounds recorded by the protagonists go through a filter of the direction. The producer and director of the project select only those materials they consider to be the ability to build the story. We can understand that the entire story is not imagined and directed by the characters, as we would have expected (at least partially), the process being controlled by this production team that leads the subject in a carefully thought out way.

 The participatory mode contributes to a unitary whole that evolves and that, theoretically, could never end (Gaudenzi 58). The continuity of a story of this kind can be achieved both by adding new materials by current subjects and by involving new characters, spaces, or actions. The volitional and plastic character of this mode of interaction shapes the ideal climate for the poetic narrative. As in previous ways, the technology used to meet the audience is the most important factor for the experimentation of poetic narrative passages to reach its maximum potential in transmitting the emotions and experiences associated with them.

5.2.4. **The experimental mode**

The "experimental mode" is the fourth and last type of interaction examined by Gaudenzi (2013) to understand how interactive documentation occurs/happens. This mode refers to the developments that occur in the media focused on geographical positioning through the use of mobile technologies. In this way, the user experience becomes affected by the particularities of the place, being in a continuous transformation (day-night differences, crowded or not traffic, weather, etc.), in contrast to the hypertext mode, fixed algorithm, which is developed under precisely defined and set conditions. If with hypertext or participatory documentaries the interaction took place through an electronic device that can be used in any space, the viewer accesses content connected by GPS technology to a particular space. Thus, the experience of consuming an audiovisual product that may or may not have a direct link to a particular place is shaped by the process of spatial positioning. Of course, not only the positioning itself is of paramount importance; it also depends on how it plays the audiovisual material is used - video projector (2D, 3D), LED screen, tablet, phone, etc., as well as the time of day or the current season (if it is an outdoor space).

A concrete example is the documentary Rider Spoke (2007) which invites the public to cycle through the streets of London. More information about this project can be found in the official description on the company's website:

"After a brief introduction and safety information, take to the streets with a laptop computer mounted on the handlebars. You will be asked a question and you will be invited to look for a suitable hiding place where you will record your answer. The device screen acts primarily as a positioning system, showing where you are and if there are hiding places nearby.

Once you find a hiding place (a place previously undiscovered by another player), the device will light an alert and a question. The question is a selection written by The Blast Theory, which asks you to be alone, in an atypical place - to reflect on your life. Then record the answer on the device.

The other aspect of the game is to find the hidden places of others. When you find one, the device warns you to stop and then shows you the question that person answered and answers your answer. The recordings that people make are only available in this context: played by a player, alone, instead of in which they were registered.

As you move through the streets, the focus shifts outward, looking for good places to hide, speculating about the hidden places of others, becoming completely immersed in this overlapping world, while the voices of strangers draw you to a new place and unknown."

(Rider Spoke)

The strong point of the experimental mode is precisely the fact that it puts us in direct relation with the surrounding space. We become aware and, at the same time, metacognitive concerning what space and the world around us means to us.

Other modes of interaction, as we have seen before, place us differently in the reality they want to portray. But, using one mode of interactivity rather than another, each interactive documentary provides a specific network of connections that direct our actions and therefore place us in a certain type of relationship with our world (Gaudenzi).

We discover, through the analysis of the presented way, that this type of project favors the poetic documentaries in their development. The unique, subjective experience, focused on emotions, puts us in direct connection with what the author wants us to feel, live, learn. The connection through space is a connection that requires more senses than the auditory-visual ones. We can touch the wind, the warm-cold air, we can hear 360 degrees and see without technological help, we can taste a certain food, a certain drink, we can feel the specific smell of space without being limited by technology.

The types of experiences listed become some of the most challenging and intriguing sides of immersive cinema. We are seeing, in recent years, an explosion of augmented reality technologies. Various innovations come together to achieve a more real experience, as intense as possible for the viewer. The more realistically the viewer's senses are stimulated, the more transparent the interaction between man and technology becomes, the immersive capacity of the poetic documentary will lead the viewer into an immersion that will increasingly resemble the initial vision of filmmakers.

Like any other mode of interaction, it also develops several vulnerabilities. If the interaction with space can stimulate us more creatively by involving more senses in this process, the inevitable parasitism of the space in which the action takes place (if the action takes place in public spaces or changes its appearance within a short time) with elements that are not part of the initial story, can bring a plus or a minus to the immersive documentary. For example, a car accident on a certain street or an insistent alarm sound of a parked car can distract us so that we miss important details from the immersive experience in which we engaged.

The poetic documentary depends on all these transformations, be they socio-political, technological, or cultural. The immersive world in which society is anchored day by day is becoming an alternative to reality - which documentary filmmakers have tried to represent throughout history. The poet has, therefore, the chance to be reborn and become a dominant way in this age of information that gives us more and more difficult the time and space necessary to live the exclusivity of a sensory experience.

Conclusions

The documentary film will undergo structural, compositional, genre, stylistic changes, along with the technological evolution and the visual language, but it will remain, in essence, a didactic genre and at the same time a cinematic form eager for exploration and knowledge. Throughout this paper, I have constantly emphasized that the documentary is only a representation of real situations, and this representation is subject to a process of transformation, manipulation, and development.

After looking, in Chapter 1, at a parallel between the reality represented in the classical visual arts and the reality represented in the poetic documentary, we can understand the major influence that the modes of representation have on this type of documentary. As we have noticed, the real and the relation to the real represent the cornerstone of the documentary film in general and the poetic mode in particular. Thus, this way of recycling the ideas, concepts, principles, which have been the basis of the visual arts since antiquity, becomes the bridge between the new media and the aesthetics of the poetic documentary.

A little later, in Chapter 2, we treated not only the birth of documentary as a genre but also how the poetic documentary carves a specific aesthetic. Nanook from the North, the one who emphasized the importance of directing in documentary film, throws us into a hybrid area, borrowing elements from fiction film, while deepening experimental, poetic, or even non-narrative lines. It is becoming increasingly clear in our research that the documentary is not the holder of the absolute truth, as propaganda films try to convince us, nor will it be a strip of reality, despite the attempts of those who have worked in direct cinema, ciné-vérité or observational. All in

Chapter 2, we showed how technological innovations have managed to destroy the monopoly of large production houses through the reliability of video editing programs, video cameras, and online distribution platforms. Another advantage of modern technologies, which I discovered in my research, also refers to the measurability of reactions, preferences real-time audience.

The importance of this chapter is underlined by the transformations of chemistry between the audience and the documentary. Relating the public to the type of film product targeted by this research is essential for paradigm shifts to be beneficial to the production process. We noticed how documentarians become independent of large production companies, but, at the same time, dependent on the public and market trends.

From Chapter 3 it is important to remember that although documentaries appear in a wide range of representations, they often have aesthetic, compositional, rhythmic similarities. Just as in fiction films we find a whole arsenal of genres in which they are divided, the contrast between them is rendered, in essence, by the directorial vision of the filmmaker involved in making the film. No matter how hard he tries to create a narrative, non-narrative structure, or an original style, certain basic features cannot work without being part of an already existing pattern. Therefore, a parallel study between aesthetics and the evolution of other ways of the documentary, but also experimental films or essays, shows us the process through which the aesthetics of poetic documentary evolved,

Chapters 4 and 5 are of great importance because during these chapters the poetic documentaries are analyzed structurally and compositionally, the main theme of this work. It is important to remember how the global interconnection, the anthropic imprint left on the planetary scale, is outlined as a theme throughout modern poetic documentaries and how they manage, through music, rhythm, image, and atypical visual compositions, to capture life in its raw form.

The production of the documentary film is done in a relatively similar way to that of the fiction film. During the ciné-vérité currents or direct cinema, filmmakers created films in a more disorganized manner, preferring an area of intimacy, the natural.

Today, documentaries are largely built on previously written screenplays and a well-organized production. The filming, production, editing team, including reconstructions written by fiction writers, line by line, of some events in concrete life, make us question the veracity of the information presented in the mainstream and beyond.

Beyond these aspects, peeling the aesthetics of poetic documentaries and analyzing it through the method of the case study or document analysis, we noticed how these documentaries respect a specific structure and how the elements of this structure have universal applicability, in the case of poetic documentaries, thing demonstrated by the comparative study performed.

At the same time, we pointed out, in Chapter 5, how the aesthetics of the poetic documentary evolve in relation to the new technologies. We analyzed the connection between poetic documentaries and other emerging technologies, highlighting the contributions of the most important theorists in the field of interest. The classification of the new modes of interaction between documentary and public film, which appeared with the technological evolution, comes as a complement to Nichols' theory that refers only to the classification of documentaries in the classic format. After careful research, we realize that poetic documentaries not only cover the versatility of the possibilities of new technologies but become an important way of representing reality in relation to the new types of documentaries analyzed.

To demonstrate this versatility and universality of the specific elements of poetic documentary aesthetics, during Chapter 6 I developed a comprehensive case study on the video project entitled Persistence of Memory made by me as a valuable complement to my research. Through this practical project, we demonstrated the applicability of aesthetic elements in the construction of a poetic documentary, following the specific production stages. Thus, most of the elements debated through case studies, document analysis, contradiction method, or transdisciplinarity (combining the theory of visual arts aesthetics with the theory of documentary film aesthetics) become sustainable as archetypes, which can be extracted from the sphere of theoretical conceptualization and used as points of departure in the construction of future poetic documentaries.

Bibliography
Studies on the documentary film

Aitken, Ian. Encyclopedia of the Documentary Film 3-Volume Set. New York: Routledge, 2005.

Aufderheide, Patricia. Documentary Film: A Very Short Introduction. Oxford: Oxford University Press, 2007.

Austin, Thomas, and De Jong, Wilma. Rethinking Documentary: New Perspectives, New Practices. Maidenhead: Open University Press, 2008.

Barnouw, Erik. Documentary: A History of the Non-Fiction Film. London: Oxford University Press, 1993.

Bazin, André. What is the Cinema? Vol. 1, Bucharest: UNATC Press, 2014.

Bordwell, David. "The Art Cinema as a Mode of Film Practice." Film Criticism, vol 4, no. 1, 1979, pp. 56–64. JSTOR, jstor.org/stable/44018650. --- " Montage in Soviet Art and Film." Cinema Journal, vol. 11, no. 2, 1972, pp. 9–17. JSTOR, jstor.org/stable/1225046.

Bordwell, David, and Kristin Thompson. Film art: an introduction. Ed. 8, New York: McGraw-Hill, 2008.

Bromhead, Toni de. Looking Two Ways: Documentaries Relationship with Cinema and reality. Intervention Press, 1996.

Bunuel, Luis. My Last Sigh. Minneapolis: University Of Minnesota Press, 2003.

Clayton, Koppes and Black, Gregory. Hollywood Goes to War. New York: The Free Press,1987.

Corciovescu, Cristina, and Bujor Râpeanu. A century of Cinematography, Small encyclopedia of universal cinematography. Bucharest: Scientific and Encyclopedic Publishing House, 1989.

Cousins, Mark and Macdonald, Kevin. Imagining Reality. London: Faber and Faber Limited, 2006.

Damian, Laurențiu. Documentary film. About the documentary ... One more thing. Bucharest: Technical Publishing House, 2003.

De la Peña, Nonny, et al. "Immersive Journalism: Immersive Virtual Reality for the FirstPerson Experience of News." Presence: Teleoperators and Virtual Environments, vol 19, no. 4, MIT Press - Journals, Aug. 2010, pp. 291-301. CrossRef,

DOI: 10.1162 / pres_a_00005.

We are, Sandra. The Living Documentary: from representing reality to co-creating reality in a digital interactive documentary. London: University of London, 2013.

Gray, Hugh. "Robert Flaherty and the Naturalistic Documentary." Hollywood Quarterly (1950): Vol. 5, No. 1, pp. 41-48.

Hitler, Adolf. My fight. trad. Calin, Joshua. Craiova: Beladi Publishing House, 1999.

Klotman, Phyllis Rauch and Cutler, Janet. Struggles for Representation: African American

Documentary Film and Video. Bloomington: Indiana University Press, 1999.

Landesman, Ohad. "In and out of this world: digital video and the aesthetics of realism in the new hybrid documentary". Studies in Documentary Film, Vol. 2, No. 1, 2008, pp.33-45.

Little, John Arthur. The Power and Potential of Performative Documentary Film. Bozeman: Montana State University, 2007.

MacDonald, Scott. A Critical Cinema 5: Interviews with Independent Filmmakers. Ed. 1, University of California Press, 2006.

--- "Avant-Doc: Eight Intersections". Film Quarterly, vol. 64, no. 2, 2010, pp. 50-57. JSTOR, jstor.org/stable/10.1525/fq.2010.64.2.50.

Maier, Lucian. "Directions in the current Romanian documentary". Film policies: contributions to interpreting contemporary Romanian cinema, Cluj- Napoca: Tact Publishing House, 2014, pp. 211-233.

Majors, Michael. Truth and Lies in Cinema Truth. Washington: The Evergreen State College, 1982.

Malița, Liviu. Censorship in the sense of the censored. Bucharest: Tracus Arte, 2016.

Mamber, Stephen. Cinema Truth in America. Studies in Uncontrolled Documentary. Cambridge, Massachusetts: The MIT Press, 1974.

Monaco, James. How to Read a Film: the Art, Technology, Language, History, and Theory of Film and Media. Oxford: Oxford University Press, 1981.

Morin, Edgar. "Festival Catalog of Cinéma du Réel." Paris, 1980.

Narayanaswami, Karthik. „Analysis of Nazi Propaganda. A Behavioral Study ". HIST E 1572: Holocaust in History, Literature, and Film (no year).

Neff, Taylor. "Propaganda on the Big Screen: Film in the Soviet Union from 1925 to 1936". Aquila - The FGCU Student Research Journal, vol. 3, no. 2, 2017.

Nichols, Bill. Introduction to Documentary. Bloomington: Indiana University Press, 2001.

---. "The Voice of Documentary." Film Quarterly, vol 36, no. 3, 1983, pp. 17-30. JSTOR, jstor.org/stable/3697347.

Nisbet, Matt, and Hirsch, Karen. Documentaries on a Mission: How Nonprofits are Making Movies for Public Engagement. Washington: Center for Media & Social Impact, 2007.

Renov, Michael. Away from Copying: The Art of Documentary Practice. Bristol Intellect Books, 2007.

Ruby, Jay. "The Mirrored Image: Reflexivity and the Documentary Film". Journal of the University Film Association, vol 29, no. 4, 1977, pp. 3-11. JSTOR, www.jstor.org/stable/20687384.

Ruoff, Jeffrey. "An Ethnographic Surrealist Film: Luis Buñuel's Land Without Bread,

Hanover ". Visual Anthropology Review, vol 14, no. 1, 1998, pp. 45-57.

Russell, Michael. Soviet Montage Cinema as Propaganda and Political Rhetoric. Edinburgh: The University of Edinburgh Press, 2009.

Sapino, Roberta. What is a Documentary Film: Discussion of the Genre. Berlin: Freie University, 2011.

Saunders, Dave. Direct Cinema: Observational Documentary and the Politics of the Sixties. London: Wallflower Press, 2007.

Schoots, Hans. Living Dangerously: A Biography of Joris Ivens. Amsterdam: Amsterdam University Press, 2000.

Scott, Anthony, and Mansell, James. The Projection Of Britain: A History of the GPO Film United. London: British Film Institute, 2011.

Sfetcu, Nicolae. The Art of Movies. www.lulu.com. 01 Oct. 2011.

Stern, Frank. "Screening Politics: Cinema and Intervention." Georgetown Journal of International Affairs, vol. 1, no. 2, 2000, pp. 65-73. JSTOR, jstor.org/stable/43133408.

Sussex, Elizabeth, and Grierson, John. "Grierson on Documentary: The Last Interview." Film Quarterly, vol. 26, no. 1, 1972, pp. 24-30. JSTOR, jstor.org/stable/1211408.

Șopterean, Marius. Memory and film: Introduction to the stylistics and history of cinema. Cluj-Napoca: Clusium, 2008.

Țuțui, Marian. "The History of Romanian Film in 7000 Words." Scribd.com, 2010.

Vertov, Dziga, and Michelson, Annette. Kino-Eye: The Writings of Dziga Vertov. Berkeley: University of California Press, 1984.

VeVe A. Clark, et al. "The Legend of Maya Deren", Anthology Film Archives, vol 1, Part 2,2006.

Whalen, Zach, and Taylor, N. Playing the Past: History and Nostalgia in Video
 Games. Nashville: Vanderbilt University Press, 2008. Project MUSE.

Wakeman, John. World Film Directors. Volume One. New York: The HW Wilson
 Company, 1987.

Online resources about documentary film

Addiego, Walter. "Samsara review: no words, but a message". 07 Sep. 2012, sfgate.com/movies/article/Samsara-review-no-words-but-a-message-3844736.

Accessed 22 Jan. 2018.

Anderson-Moore, Oakley. „Nichols' 6 Modes of Documentary Might Expand Your Storytelling Strategies ". 17 Sep. 2015. nofilmschool.com/2015/09/nichols-6-modes-documentary-can-help-expand-yourstorytelling. Accessed 28 Apr. 2018.

Bonsaver, Guido. "The Aesthetics of documentary filmmaking and Giallo a Milano: An interview with film director Sergio Basso and sociologist Daniele Cologna". The Italianist, 18 Jul. 2013, www.tandfonline.com/doi/abs/10.1179/026143411X13051090964974. Accessed 22 Jan. 2018.

Biesterfeld, Peter. "Six Primary Styles of Documentary Production". 13 Nov. 2016, www.videomaker.com/article/c06/18423-six-primary-styles-of-documentaryproduction. Accessed 28 Apr. 2018.

Bucha, Ali, Raza. "Reading log on Reflexive mode of Documentary". May 31, 2015, www.mediafactory.org.au/ali-bucha. Accessed 24 Apr. 2018.

Camper, Fred. By Brakhage: The Act of Seeing. May 25, 2010, www.criterion.com/current/posts/272-by-brakhage-the-act-of-seeing. Accessed 28 Apr.2018.

Cousins, Mark. "The aesthetics of documentary ". Tits. 1 January. 2006 www.tate.org.uk/context-comment/articles/aesthetics-documentary. Accessed Jan. 20.2018.

„Catalog / Scenes From Under Childhood: Section No. 1". without a year, filmmakerscoop.com/catalogue/stan-brakhage-scenes-from-under-childhood-section-no-1. 28 Apr. 2018.

Cettl, Robert. "Powaqqatsi 1988". June 14, 2012, letterboxd.com/widerscreenings/film/powaqqatsi. Accessed 29 Apr. 2018.

Cizek, Katerina. „The Thousandth Tower. 2009 ". National Film Board Canada, highrise.nfb.ca/thousandthtower. Accessed 30 Aug. 2018.

"Confessions (2011)." Cinemagia, cinemagia.ro/filme/confessions-578560/. Accessed 10 Jan.2018.

Daniels, Jessie. "Teaching and Learning with Documentaries in the Digital Age". Oct. 22, 2010, csosnowy.pressbooks.com/chapter/teaching-and-learning-with-documentaries-inthe-digital-era. Accessed 15 Feb. 2018.

Duncan, Dean. "Nanook of the North". Jan 11, 1999, criterion.com/current/posts/42-nanookof-the-north. Accessed 14 Apr. 2018.

Eber, Rogert. "Samsara". March 12, 2012, rogerebert.com/reviews/samsara-201220. Accessed 23 Jan. 2018.

"Expository Mode. " Free year, epowdocumentary.wordpress.com/documentary-modes / expository mode. Accessed 22 Apr. 2018.

Fricke, Ron, and Magidson, Mark. „Ron Fricke & Mark Magidson and The Making of Samsara. " Aug 17, 2012, in70mm.com/news/2012/samsara/interview/uk/index.html. Accessed January 21. 2018.

Hall, Zack. "Stan Brakhage's The Act of Seeing with One's Own Eyes." March 10, 2008, lostatsea.net/feature.phtml?fid=18853449354767ab65cb6aa. Accessed 28 Apr. 2018.

Himpele, Jeff, and Castañeda, Quetzil. „A Guide to Re-View Incidents of Travel in Chichén Itzá ". Aug. 20, 2003, archive.li/NMjg6. Accessed 28 Apr. 2018.

Hoberman James Lewis. "Scenes from under Childhood". 19 we. 2008 villagevoice.com/2008/11/19/scenes-from-under-childhood. Accessed 28 Apr. 2018.

"Interactive Documentary Context". Mediafactory, 10 Aug. 2015, mediafactory.org.au/2015new-documentary/2015/08/10/interactive-documentary-context. Accessed 10 Jan. 2018.

Keenlyside, Sarah. „Festivals: Post-Sundance 2001; Docs Still Face Financing and Distribution Challenges ". 08 Feb. 2001, indiewire.com/2001/02/festivals-post-sundance2001-docs-still-face-financing-and-distribution-challenges-81142. Accessed 15 Apr. 2018.

Manov, Lev. "Whatis digital cinema?". NYU Web Publishing. September. 2013, wp.nyu.edu/novak-mm13/wp-content/uploads/sites/41/2013/09/Lev-Manovich-_Essays-_-What-is-Digital-Cinema. Accessed 13 Feb. 2018.

Mills, Ted. "Watch the Very First Feature Documentary: Nanook of the North by Robert J. Flaherty (1922)". July 15, 2015, openculture.com/2015/07/watch-the-very-first-featuredocumentary-nanook-of-the-north-byrobert-j-flaherty-1922.html. Accessed 18 Aug. 2016.

Nam, Yoommy. „Cinéma Vérité Vs. Direct Cinema: An Introduction ". 20 noi. 2005, nyfa.edu/student-resources/cinema-verite-vs-direct-cinema-an-introduction/. Accessed 14 Apr. 2018.

"Nazi And Soviet Propaganda's Shared Aesthetic". Mar 20 2013, rferl.org/a/24934238.html. Accessed 21 Apr. 2018.

"Observational Mode ". Free year. epowdocumentary.wordpress.com/documentary-modes / observational mode. Accessed 24 Apr. 2018.

Owen, Jeremy. "Contemporary Cinematic Documentary and The Rebirth of Content". MA Media, Communication & Critical Practice, no year, filmint. nu/wp-

Content / uploads / 2011/06 / j. owen_diss_final. Accessed July 22, 2018.

"Participatory and Reflexive Modes of Documentary: Response 4". 06 Nov. 2013, sites.stedwards.edu/comm4399fa2013-jhender4/2013/11/06/participatory-and-reflexivemodes-of-documentary-response-4. Accessed 24 Apr. 2018.

"Performing Documentary Characteristics ". 08 September. 2009 wemz29.wordpress.com/2009/09/08/performative-documentary-characteristics. Accessed 28 Apr. 2018.

"Rider Spoke". 2007, blasttheory.co.uk/projects/rider-spoke. Accessed 30 Aug. 2018.

Rohter, Larry. "What's Real gets More Creative ". 14 Apple. 2014 nytimes.com/2014/03/16/movies/the-missing-picture-and-other-films rethinkdocumentaries.html. Accessed May 15, 2018.

Ryan, Marie-Laure. "Narrative and the Split Condition of Digital Textuality". 2005, dichtung-digital.de/2005/1/Ryan. July 20, 2018.

Shlain, Tiffany. "The Cloud Filmmaking Manifesto ". 12 April. 2012 tribecafilm.com/stories/513618fe1c7d76b51b0000 13-the-cloud-filmmaking-mani.

Accessed May 25, 2018.

Smith Simon. "Movie Review: Powaqqatsi". 14 July. 2010 higherplainmusic.com/2010/07/14/film-review-powaqqatsi. Accessed 29 Apr. 2018.

Spiegel, Josh. "Samsara is a meticulous, beautiful documentary of the core of humanity." Sep 14 2012, popoptiq.com/samsara-is-a-meticulous-beautiful-documentary-of-the-coreof-humanity. Accessed 30 April. 2018.

vice, Jeff. "Movie review: Naqoyqatsi". 07 April. 2003 deseretnews.com/article/700003198/Naqoyqatsi.html. Accessed 29 Apr. 2018.

Wilkie, Ben. "Review: Koyaanisqatsi Live (Philip Glass Ensemble)". March 12, 2017. limelightmagazine.com.au/reviews/review-koyaanisqatsi-live-philip-glass-ensemble. Accessed 29 Apr. 2018.

Wood, Daniel. "In 'docu-ganda' films, balance is not the aim." June 2, 2006, csmonitor.com/2006/0602/p01s02-ussc.html. Accessed 15 Apr. 2018.

Aesthetic studies and art theory

Achim, Ionel, et al. Dictionary of general aesthetics, Bucharest: Politică Publishing House, 1972.

Aslam, Constantin. Aesthetics course paradigms of art and beauty from a historical and systematic perspective. Bucharest: National University of Arts, 2006.

Baudelaire, Charles. Aesthetic curiosities. Bucharest: Meridian Publishing House, 1971.

Bürger, Peter. Theory of the Avant-Garde. Minneapolis: University of Minnesota Press, 1984.

Grammer, Karl, and Thornhill, Randy. „Human (Homo Sapiens) Facial Attractiveness and Sexual Selection: The Role of Symmetry and Averageness ". Journal of Comparative Psychology, vol. 108, no. 3, American Psychological Association (APA), 1994, pp. 233242. Crossref, DOI: 10.1037 / 0735-7036.108.3.233.

Genette, Gérard. Introduction to architecture. Bucharest: Univers Publishing House, 1979.

Hegel, Charles Bénard, and Bryant, WM. M. "Hegel On Classic Art". The Journal of Speculative Philosophy, vol 12, no. 2, 1878, 145-160. JSTOR. jstor.org/stable/pdf/25666080.pdf?refreqid=search%3A7ad975d198fe92a75001960bf 56cf1b7.

Honor, Hugh, and Fleming, John. The Visual Arts: A History. 4th Edition, Englewood Cliffs: NJ: Prentice-Hall, 1995.

Kristeller, Paul Oskar. "The Modern System of the Arts: A Study in the History of Aesthetics (II)." Journal of the History of Ideas, vol. 13, no. 1, 1952, pp. 17-46. JSTOR, jstor.org/stable/2707724.

Norris, Michael, and others. Medieval Art: A Resource for Educators. New York: The Metropolitan Museum of Art, 2005.

Moles, Abraham. Scientific creation. Geneva: René Kister, 1957.

Osborne, H. „Color Concepts of the Ancient Greeks". British Journal of Aesthetics, Vol.8, no. 3 1968.

Raditsa, Bosiljka, and others. The Art of Renaissance Europe: A Resource for Educators. New York: The Metropolitan Museum of Art, 2000.

Renato, Poggioli. The Theory of the Avant-Garde. Cambridge: Belknap Press of Harvard University, 1981.

Roussel-Despierres, François. "The Aesthetic Ideal". The Art World, vol. 1, no. 6, 1917, 429-432. JSTOR, jstor.org/stable/pdf/25587824.pdf?refreqid=excelsior%3A06b5fd95d415e99dc4f1b12 8318c6eb0.

Schapiro, Meyer. Impressionism: Reflections and Perceptions. New York: Columbia University Press, 1997.

Urmă, Maria. „The Perspective in Ancient Greece an Original Way of Constituting the Spatial Composition ". Distortion Journal, vol. 11, 2008-2009.

Walter, Benjamin. The work of art in the era of its technical reproducibility. Cluj-Napoca: Tact Publishing, 2012.

Online resources: aesthetics and art theory

"Art of Renaissance and Baroque Europe ". Free date, wwnorton.com/college/art/gatewaystoart/ch/26/ebook.aspx. Accessed 22 Jan. 2018.

Celkyte, Aiste. Ancient Aesthetics. Yonsei University, No date, iep.utm.edu/ancaest/#H1. Accessed July 22, 2017.

"Classical Color Palette". No date, visual-arts-cork.com/artist-paints/classical-colourpalette.htm. Accessed 05 Aug. 2017.

"C003: Greek Art theory and style". Royal Society of Chemistry, undated, rsc.org/learnchemistry/content/filerepository/CMP/00/006/296/C003%20Greek%20Art%20Theor y.pdf. Accessed July 25, 2017.

Chandler, Daniel. "semiotics forum Beginners'. Free date, visual memory.co.uk/daniel/Documents/S4B/sem01.html. Accessed 12 Feb. 2018.

Erzen, Jale. "Aesthetics versus Beauty". No date. ritsumei.ac.jp/acd/re/krsc/lcs/kiyou/pdf_25-1/RitsIILCS_25.1pp.9-15Jale Erzen.pdf.

Faur Christian. "The semiotics of Color ". Free date. christianfaur.com/color/Site/Color%20Semiotics.html. Accessed 12 Apr. 2018.

"Greek Sculpture. The Rise of Realism ". Essential Humanities, undated, www.essentialhumanities.net/western-art/sculpture/greek. Accessed July 22, 2017.

"Greek Symbols and Their related meanings ". Free date, ancient-symbols.com/greek_symbols.html. Accessed 05 Aug. 2017.

Glossary Of Rouchian Terms. No date, maitres-fous.net/glossary.html. Accessed 17 Feb.2018.

Hemingway, Seán, and Hemingway, Colette. "The Art of Classical Greece (ca. 480-323 BC)". Department of Greek and Roman Art, The Metropolitan Museum of Art, Jan. 2008, metmuseum.org/toah/hd/tacg/hd_tacg.htm. Accessed July 25. 2017.

"The Meaning of Greek Art". No date, greek-thesaurus.gr/classical-period-greek-art.html. Accessed July 22, 2017.

Marder, Lisa. "Impressionism and Photography ". 06 Apple. 2017 thoughtco.com/impressionism-and-photography-2578247. Accessed Jan. 29. 2018.

Nenova, Stella. "The Colors of the Ancient Greeks and Romans." Ancient World Alive. June 8, 2017, ancientworldalive.com/single-post/2017/06/08/The-Colors-of-the Ancient-Greeks-and-Romans. Accessed July 29, 2017.

Tanner, Norman P. The Papal Encyclicals Online. No date. papalencyclicals.net/councils/ecum01.htm. Accessed January 21. 2018.

Warburton, David Alan. "Ancient Color Categories". Encyclopedia of Color Science and Technology, July 29. 2014, imbs.uci.edu/~kjameson/ECST/Warbuton_AncientColorCategories. Accessed July 24, 2016.

Other printed resources

Barber, Benjamin. Fear's Empire: War, Terrorism, and Democracy. New York: WW Norton & Co, 2004.

Chadwick, Andrew, and Howard, Philip N. Routledge handbook of Internet politics. London & New York: Routledge, 2009.

Deleuze, Gilles. Cinema 1. Motion-image. Translated by Ştefana and Ioan Pop-Curşeu. Cluj-Napoca: Editura Tact, 2012.

Gorzo, Andrei. Images framed in history: The century of Miklós Jancsó. Cluj-Napoca: Tact Publishing House, 2015.

---. Things that can't be said otherwise: A way of thinking about cinema, from André Bazin to Cristi Puiu. Bucharest: Humanitas, 2012.

Smarandache, Ligia. The role of the video essay in postmodern audiovisual communication. Cluj-Napoca: University of Art and Design, 2011.

Other online resources

Manea, Irina Maria. "Charlemagne, a promoter of the cultural renaissance." Without date, historia.ro/sectiune/portret/articol/carol-cel-mare-un-promotor-al-renasterii-culturale. Accessed January 21. 2018.

Morozov, Evgeny. "Political Repression 2.0". The New York Times, Sept. 1, 2011, nytimes.com/2011/09/02/opinion/political-repression-2-0.html. Accessed 13 Oct. 2018.

Roser, Max, and Ortiz-Ospina, Esteban. Global Rise of Education. Our World in Data, ourworldindata.org/global-rise-of-education. Accessed 22 Oct. 2018.

Stevens, Dana. "For the Iraqis Interviewed, Daily Life Is Better Today." Feb 29 2004, nytimes.com/2004/10/29/movies/for-the-iraqis-interviewed-daily-life-is-bettertoday.html. Accessed 15 Feb. 2018.

Filmography

Arora Gabo, and Milk, Chris, directors. Waves of Grace. VRSE, 2015 youtube.com/watch?v=0lwG6MfGvwI&t=94s. Accessed May 27. 2019.

Brakhage, Stan, director. Window Water Baby Moving. Independent film, 1959, youtube.com/watch?v=Q_MA8h8PXQM. Accessed March 15. 2019.

--- The Act of Seeing with One's Own Eyes. Movie independent, 1971 youtube.com/watch?v=KbVTtHYbWog. Accessed March 15. 2019.

--- Scenes from under Childhood. Movie independent, 1967-1970, youtube.com/watch?v=GBRajt7f9WU. Accessed March 17. 2019.

Berger, John, director. The Ways of Seeing. British Broadcasting Corporation, 1972.

Buñuel Luis, director. Land without Bread. Ramon Acin, 1932 youtube.com/watch?v=vUmmfYagWDA. Accessed March 17. 2019.

Carson, Greg, director. The Essence of Life. MGM Home Entertainment, 2002.

Chang, Mandy, director. The Camera That Changed the World. BBC Channel 4, 2011.

Chierego, Marta, director. The Fourth Industrial Revolution. The World Economic Forum, 2016, vimeo.com/182738685. Accessed March 17. 2019.

Ciulei, Thomas, director. That's it. Ciulei Films, 2001, youtube.com/watch?v=RdZuHPjJtgs. Accessed March 17. 2019.

Clarke, Shirley, director. Portrait of Jason. Milestone Films, 1967.

Colbert, Gregory, director. Ashes and Snow. Flying Elephants Productions, 2005.

Craig, Gilbert, producer. An American Family. Public Broadcasting Service, 1973.

Dăscălescu Andrew, director. Constantin and Elena. Filmlab, 2009 youtube.com/watch?v=R6pd5aVMLzs. Accessed March 25. 2018.

Deren, Maya, and Hammid, Alexander, directors. The Private Fife of a Cat. Independent film, 1947, youtube.com/watch?v=QpR_UZz-BS4. Accessed March 17. 2019.

--- Meshes of the Afternoon, Independent film, 1943, youtube.com/watch?v=ihQurg4xGcI. Accessed March 17. 2019.

Eisenstein, Serghei. Potemkin Cruiser. London: British Film Institute, 1925. youtube.com/watch?v=_4Qfuzn25sI. Accessed March 20. 2019.

Eisenstein, Serghei and Aleksandrov, Grigori, directors. October. Sovkino, 1928.

Flaherty, Robert, director. Nanook from the North. International Film Seminars, 1976, youtube.com/watch?v=m4kOIzMqso0. Accessed March 17. 2019.

--- The man from Aran. Gainsborough Pictures, 1934, youtube.com/watch?v=Rk9tTyG0gcY. Accessed March 25. 2019.

Fox, Beryl, director. The Mills of the Gods: Viet Nam. Canadian Broadcasting Corporation,1965.

Fricke, Ron, director. Chronos. Les Productions de la Géode, 1985.

Grierson, John, Wright, Basil, and Watt, Harry, directors. Night Mail. London: The GPO Film United, 1936, youtube.com/watch?v=sLFv6CutWzI. Accessed March 17. 2019.

Ivens, Joris, director. Regen. Movie independent, 1929 youtube.com/watch?v=6ADNWzg4ZmE. Accessed March 8. 2019.

Jacquet, Luc, director. The Emperor's Way. Wild Bunch, National Geographic Films, 2005.

Kunert, Martin, director. Voices of Iraq. Magnolia Pictures, 2004.

Lumière, Louis, director. The sprinkler. Paris: Société Lumière, 1895, youtube.com/watch?v=looPPi1YzkM. Accessed March 8. 2019.

--- Exit of the Workers from the Lumière Factories. Paris: Société Lumière, 1895, youtube.com/watch?v=DEQeIRLxaM4. Accessed May 12. 2019.

Lumière, Louis and Lumière, Auguste, directors. A train at the station at Ciotat. Paris: Société Lumière, 1895, youtube.com/watch?v=1dgLEDdFddk. Accessed May 12. 2019.

Macdonald, Kevin, director. Life in a Day, Scott Free Productions, 2011, youtube.com/watch?v=JaFVr_cJJIY&t=1428s. Accessed May 12. 2019.

Marker, Chris, director. Without the Sun. Argos Film, 1983.

McElwee, Ross, director. Photographic Memory. St Quay Films, 2011.

Minh-ha, Trinh, director. Surname Viet Nam. 1989.

Moore, Michael, et al., Directors. Fahrenheit 9/11. Culver City, Calif.: Columbia TriStar Home Entertainment, 2004.

Morin, Edgar, and Rouch, Jean, directors. Chronicle of a summer. Argos Films, 1961.

Reggio, Godfrey, director. Koyaanisqatsi. New Cinema and Island Alive, 1983.

--- Naqoyqatsi. Miramax Films, 2002.

--- Powaqqatsi. Golan-Globus, 1988.

Riggs, Marlon, director. Untied tongs. Frameline & California Newsreel, 1989.

Rouch, Jean, director. The Crazy Masters. Documentary Educational Resources, 1954, youtube.com/watch?v=Z8uHE2oIARk. Accessed May 12. 2019.

Ruttmann, Walther, director. Berlin, the Symphony of a Great City. Blackhawk Films, 1924, youtube.com/watch?v=0NQglvG-kBM. Accessed May 12. 2019.

Smarandache, Ligia, director. Confessions. University of Arts and Design, 2011, youtube.com/watch?v=yIfiAzvC5N0. Accessed May 12. 2019.

Teller, Joseph, director. Tim's Vermeer. High Delft Pictures, 2013.

"The Blue Planet." Moderated by David Attenborough, BBC, 2001.

Ucicky, Gustav director. Heimkehr. Universum Movie AG 1941 youtube.com/watch?v=jhqrz5wvo_U. Accessed May 27. 2019.

Ujica, Andrei, director. The autobiography of Nicolae Ceaușescu. ICON production, 2010, youtube.com/watch?v=6LvsJlGJ5Go. Accessed May 12. 2019.

Vertov, Dziga, director. Man with a Movie Camera. 1929 youtube.com/watch?v=cGYZ5847FiI. Accessed May 27. 2019.

Vlad, Alexandru, director. We Fly Again. Faculty of Theater and Television, 2016.

Wiseman, Frederick, director. Hospital. 1970.

Other video resources

"DP / 30: Samsara, filmmakers Ron Fricke & Mark Magidson". DP / 30: The Oral History Of Hollywood. 2012, youtube.com/watch?v=-y_ddojVDY0. Accessed July 12. 2018.

"Interview with Ron Fricke and Mark Magidson ". Earth 2.0 2012 youtube.com/watch?v=pqjvvfXPRcQ. Accessed June 25, 2018.

"Propaganda / Social Engineering - Modern Practical Applications - Documentary". Proper Gander, 2016, youtube.com/watch?v=ffukW1Uqf9E. Accessed June 7, 2018.

"The History of Sound at the Movies ". Filmmaker IQ. 2014 youtube.com/watch?v=Ot5IryUt9SM. Accessed July 20. 2018.

"Towards Immersive Journalism: The IPSRESS Experience." Nonny de la Peña, 2009, youtube.com/watch?v=_z8pSTMfGSo. Accessed July 10. 2018.

www.ingramcontent.com/pod-product-compliance
Lightning Source LLC
Chambersburg PA
CBHW060826220526
45466CB00003B/993